Living a Life of Inner Harmony

MD Sharr

Published by pinky, 2025.

LIVING A LIFE OF INNER HARMONY

First edition. January 27, 2025.

ISBN: 979-8230613374

Written by MD Sharr.

Table of Contents

Preface

This book was born out of a simple hope. Many people search for calm in a world that often feels hectic. They want a life that does not revolve around constant stress or conflict. They sense there must be a kinder way to move through challenges. Yet, it can be hard to find that balance when daily pressures crowd the mind. Work deadlines press in. Family duties multiply. Disagreements flare without warning. Emotions swing from anger to regret to doubt. Even small tasks can feel exhausting when the spirit is not at ease. Faced with these struggles, some might believe inner peace is only for those who live in remote settings or devote all their time to meditation. But that is not true. This book was written to show that calm can grow in ordinary lives. It can sprout in the middle of a busy morning or an uncertain evening. It does not require special robes or years of silence. It asks only that we open our minds and hearts to a new approach. It is a path that invites us to shift how we see ourselves and others. It suggests that, by paying attention to small choices each day, we can nurture an unshakable center of peace.

The chapters in this book each touch on a vital aspect of what it means to seek inner harmony. You will find discussions about dreaming peace and how imagination can spark hope. You will see how gratitude shapes our outlook, lifting us from constant complaint to a place of sincere appreciation. You will discover the power of hope to light our path in times of despair. You will read about kindness and how small acts can unite communities. You will explore boundless love, a love that extends beyond close circles and embraces all. You will learn the strength that comes from patience, and how it can keep us steady when the urge to rush overwhelms you. You will witness the grace of inner peace itself, and how it can serve as a guiding star in times of stress. You will see how respect can mend frayed bonds, how anger can be transformed into a constructive force, and how ego can be

1

unmasked so that we embrace humility. You will also find lessons on facing fear, letting go of what binds us, releasing regrets that weigh us down, building harmony within, and finally weaving all these ideas together into a peaceful journey.

All of these themes fit under the same umbrella: our quest to live with less turmoil and more compassion. The book was written to address the everyday tensions that steal our joy. It shows that genuine peace does not require perfection or a life free of conflict. It thrives in how we respond to what comes our way. For too long, many have assumed that inner calm belongs to mystics or saints. They imagine that for normal people, chaos is just part of life. This book argues otherwise. It reminds us that we can choose small steps to foster calm each day. Over time, these steps become habits. They reshape our thoughts and emotions. They help us handle setbacks without spiraling. They help us communicate with empathy instead of judgment.

Readers might wonder why they should spend time on these pages. The answer is that peace is not a minor detail. It affects every dimension of our experiences. When we lack calm, arguments flare more often. Stress undermines our health. We might lose sight of what matters most, chasing fleeting goals or bending under social pressure. We might waste energy on resentments that never heal. In contrast, when we cultivate calm, we engage in life more fully. We respond to conflicts with clarity. We keep our wits about us when trouble hits. Our relationships grow stronger because we bring less tension into them. We also find more stability in ourselves, making decisions with a steady mind. This leads to outcomes that feel balanced, even when they are not perfect. That sense of balance can then ripple out to friends, family, and strangers we meet. It can reduce the harshness that often poisons social interactions. In a world where headlines stoke fear and division, each act of calm can serve as a small beacon. We do not need to fix every big crisis overnight. But if enough people foster inner peace, it can alter the overall climate of stress and negativity.

Another reason to read this book is that many of us carry wounds from the past. We regret decisions, we hold onto anger, or we feel stuck. Addressing those issues requires more than a quick tip. The chapters here offer in-depth explorations of how to face regret, release tension, and transform negative emotions. They provide guidance on how to treat ourselves with kindness so that healing becomes possible. They also show how patience, gratitude, or hope can lighten old burdens. None of these approaches claim to remove pain instantly. Instead, they guide the process of understanding and letting go. Each section helps us see a broader perspective. That perspective can ease the fear that often keeps us trapped in old patterns.

This book stands as a resource for practical application. It is not meant to be skimmed once and then set aside. Each chapter invites reflection. Readers can pause after a few paragraphs and think about their own experiences. They can test the ideas in real life, perhaps by using a tip on gratitude at home or employing a patience exercise at work. The beauty of these themes is that they adapt to all sorts of situations. A busy parent can practice small acts of kindness and see how it changes family meals. A student who feels anxious about exams can try letting go of perfectionism and discovering new freedom to learn. A manager facing tough calls can lean on respect and calm dialogue, noticing less friction among the team. The concepts here are universal enough to fit any role or stage of life.

Another question might be about authenticity. Are these chapters just feel-good words, or do they stem from real challenges faced by real people? While the book does not rely on personal stories in detail, the lessons were shaped by experiences shared across many places and times. The ideas about anger, fear, ego, or regret come from the human condition itself. Countless individuals have tried to conquer anger, only to realize that it must be transformed from within. Many have battled fear and discovered the courage that emerges when it is faced. These insights are woven into each chapter, creating a tapestry of lived wisdom. The aim is not to deliver rigid rules but to spark your insight. You might find that one chapter speaks louder than the rest, based on your current struggles. That is natural. The journey to inner peace is never identical for two people. We each hold unique stories. Yet, we also share similar longings for a calmer heart and a gentler world.

If you choose to read these pages, consider doing so at a pace that feels right for you. Some might prefer to read one chapter per day, letting the themes sink in. Others might read in larger portions, and then revisit certain sections later. You might keep a journal by your side, jotting down any thoughts or feelings that arise. You might also share ideas with a friend or family member, discussing how to apply them in everyday life. By engaging with the material actively, you allow it to shape your habits. A simple reflection or practice each day can plant seeds of lasting change. Over weeks or months, those seeds can grow into a more consistent sense of ease. And from that ease, new possibilities emerge.

In writing this book, the hope was to offer a gentle companion for anyone feeling weighed down by stress or confusion. It acknowledges that life has sharp edges and rough patches. But it also asserts that we carry an innate capacity for calm. We can bring that calm forward if we choose. It might show up in how we breathe during a tense moment, or how we respond to an insult with measured words instead of anger. It might appear in how we forgive ourselves for past errors, using them to guide future choices. It might flourish in acts of compassion, large or small, that remind us of our shared humanity. Each of these reflections can shape the course of our days.

Ultimately, the reason to read this book is that inner peace can transform existence from the inside out. When we become calmer, we see the world with clearer eyes. We notice small wonders we once overlooked. We connect more sincerely with people, animals, and nature. We appreciate the simple goodness around us. This does not remove sadness or heartbreak, but it provides a steady anchor. We learn to ride the waves of emotion without capsizing. We gain resilience and also a sense of spaciousness. That spaciousness allows curiosity, empathy, and joy to flourish. And these qualities are what so many of us crave when we feel battered by daily news or personal hurdles. By taking these chapters to heart, we can gradually shift from a cycle of stress to a cycle of renewal. It will not be instant or free of effort, but the path is there. The door is open. One step at a time, we can cultivate a mind and heart that dwells in peace more often than in turmoil.

As you begin your reading, keep in mind that each chapter is part of a larger mosaic. You might resonate with some chapters more than others. That is fine. This book is meant to be a supportive guide, not a strict formula. Take what helps you, experiment, and observe the effects. Return to the sections that speak to your current challenges. Over time, you may find yourself weaving bits of gratitude, hope, patience, kindness, or letting go of your daily routine. That is where the real transformation unfolds. It is in those ordinary moments—making breakfast, commuting to work, talking with a friend—that the lessons can breathe and grow. May these pages uplift your spirit and remind you that, even in a chaotic world, a gentle path is waiting for you. It waits in your choices, your thoughts, your willingness to turn toward peace again and again. Thank you for choosing to pick up this book. May it serve as a calm companion on your journey toward a more peaceful and grounded life.

—Author

1. Dreaming Peace

P eace is something many people long for, yet it often feels distant. We think about it when we see conflicts on the news or in our own lives. We wonder if there is a place where no arguments exist. We dream of a moment when everyone understands one another. This dream of peace can fill the heart with hope. It can also feel like a shining light in dark times. But how do we truly embrace this dream? For many, the first step comes in imagining a world without anger or hatred. This dream begins as a tiny spark in the mind. Then, with care, it grows. It can change our thoughts and actions. It can spread to others who also wish for calm and unity. Dreaming peace is not a weak or naive idea. It can shape how we see life and guide us to become kinder and more compassionate.

The idea of dreaming of peace is often overlooked. Some believe that real change must come from laws or strict policies. They see dreams as a fantasy. But history shows us that dreams can spark powerful movements. When people dream of something better, they find fresh ideas. These ideas might seem bold or unrealistic at first. Yet they can inspire large groups of people to act. Think of the times when communities came together to protest unfair treatment. Their shared dream gave them courage. They refused to accept the status quo. In many cases, that vision led to positive outcomes. Dreaming peace is not just daydreaming or wishing. It is a proactive step. It requires faith in human goodness. It also involves patience. It asks us to believe that every person can be touched by compassion. It tells us that violence is not the only answer.

On a personal level, dreaming of peace can bring a sense of calm. When we imagine a peaceful scenario, our minds can relax. This mental picture can help reduce anxiety. It can also guide us away from negative thoughts. Many people practice visualization as part of meditation. They picture serene scenes. Sometimes they think of a quiet meadow or a sunset on a calm ocean. This image helps them stay present and grounded. Over time, this peaceful dream can influence daily life. We might find ourselves reacting differently in tense situations. Instead of lashing out, we pause. We remember the stillness we experienced in our minds. This shift in attitude can affect the people around us. They notice our calm demeanor. They might wonder how we keep our balance. Then they might try to find a similar path. In this way, one dream can ripple out into the world.

Dreaming of peace also has a social impact that reaches beyond the individual. When a group of people shares the same dream, they create a community of hope. They gather for events and discussions. They form networks dedicated to spreading understanding. They use art and music to express their vision. Sometimes, they write stories or poems. They might paint murals or compose songs that convey the message of unity. These creative efforts can touch hearts more deeply than simple arguments. They bypass the walls people build when confronted with different opinions. Through art, the dream of peace becomes tangible. It stops being just an idea and turns into a shared experience. Communities united by this dream can influence local policies. They can encourage leaders to invest in education and dialogue. They can advocate for peaceful conflict resolution. Over time, these efforts can lead to real societal transformation.

An important element of dreaming of peace is recognizing that it does not require perfection. We all have flaws. We get angry, impatient, or frustrated at times. That does not mean the dream is lost. It is vital to remember that peace is a process. It grows stronger when we learn from our mistakes. Even when we see violence or hatred, the dream of peace can stand firm. It reminds us that there are other choices. It allows us to imagine different outcomes. In conflicts, people often believe there must be winners and losers. But when we dream of peace, we look for solutions that help everyone. We try to find common ground. We search for what unites us instead of what divides us. This mindset can transform relationships in families, workplaces, and communities. It can reduce aggression and help us positively embrace diversity.

Dreaming peace also carries great importance in a global context. Many nations have faced wars and conflicts that leave deep wounds. These scars do not vanish easily. They can pass from one generation to another, fueling anger and suspicion. Dreaming peace can be a healing force. It invites us to see people from other cultures as fellow human beings. It encourages us to understand their stories and struggles. When leaders adopt this approach, they may work harder to avoid war. They may invest in dialogue and partnerships instead of weapons. They may seek solutions to climate challenges that benefit all. This broader vision can unite countries in common goals. Although it sounds idealistic, it has happened at times in history. Nations have come together to rebuild after disasters or to protect shared resources. This cooperation is a result of dreaming of peace on a larger scale.

There are challenges to dreaming of peace. One major challenge is skepticism. Some people think it is unrealistic to focus on harmony when problems seem so large. They argue that human nature is too competitive or selfish. They believe that conflict is inevitable. Another challenge is the pressure of everyday life. People are busy trying to earn a living and support their families. They may feel they have no time to dream. They might be worried about immediate threats or difficulties. In that state, long-term visions can seem far away. Also, some groups profit from discord. They spread hateful messages or exploit tensions. They may discourage efforts towards peace. These challenges can make people doubt the power of a peaceful vision. However, when the dream is persistent, it can shine even in dark situations. It can give strength to those who refuse to let despair take over.

Another challenge is misunderstanding the concept of peace. Some think peace means avoiding all conflict or pretending problems do not exist. That is not the case. True peace acknowledges that disagreements will happen. It does not deny differences. Instead, it looks for healthy ways to resolve them. It promotes honest dialogue. It encourages empathy and respect. It urges us to see that every person has dignity. Dreaming of peace means recognizing our shared humanity. It is not about erasing cultural identities or personal beliefs. It is about finding ways to coexist without harming one another. This can be hard when emotions run high. It can be painful when past hurts are fresh. Yet the dream persists. It offers a vision of what could be. It suggests that the effort to understand one another is worthwhile. It keeps us moving forward, step by step, even when the path is not easy.

One lesser-known fact about dreaming of peace is the role of neuroscience in supporting it. Researchers have studied how visualization can change the brain's pathways. When people focus on positive images, their brains release certain chemicals. These chemicals can reduce stress and increase feelings of well-being. Over time, this practice can help a person develop more compassionate responses. Another interesting discovery is how group meditation or prayer can affect a community. Some studies claim that when many people focus on peaceful thoughts together, there are noticeable drops in local crime rates or aggression levels. Though this research is sometimes disputed, it offers intriguing insights. It suggests that collective focus might have a bigger impact than we realize. Dreaming of peace might not just be an abstract idea. It could be a real force that influences our surroundings in mysterious ways. This adds another layer of fascination to the journey.

Many spiritual traditions emphasize the power of a peaceful mind. They talk about how our inner state affects our outer world. This idea is not confined to one religion or region. It appears in teachings across the globe. Stories are told of wise individuals who found serenity within themselves. They radiated kindness in every interaction. Their presence alone could calm tensions. People who spent time with them felt a sense of ease. The dream of peace, in these teachings, starts in the heart. It moves outward in ever-widening circles. Even if we are not religious, we can find value in these practices. We can learn that our thoughts shape our emotions, and our emotions guide our actions. By holding a dream of peace in our minds, we influence how we speak, listen, and behave. This is not magic. It is simply the power of intention and consistency.

Some might wonder if dreaming of peace is the same as ignoring reality. They might think it is too simplistic. In truth, dreaming of peace often includes facing reality with courage. It means looking at the suffering in the world without turning away. It means acknowledging that people can be cruel to one another. It means understanding the roots of anger and desperation. But it also means choosing not to get stuck in despair. Instead, it suggests seeking solutions and hope. It encourages dialogue with those who are hurting or fearful. It drives campaigns to offer assistance where it is needed. It supports programs that teach empathy in schools. It funds initiatives that provide mental health care for communities. When we dream of peace, we do not hide from problems. We address them with a belief that a better way is possible. This balance of realism and hope is crucial.

In times of crisis, the dream of peace can serve as a guiding light. When chaos erupts, people may feel lost or angry. They look for someone to blame. Tensions rise quickly, and violence can feel like an easy answer. At these moments, the dream of peace reminds us to pause. It encourages leaders to seek calm. It urges communities to come together rather than fall apart. It might involve establishing safe spaces for dialogue. It could involve bringing in mediators or counselors. It might mean simply listening to each other's stories. This dream also inspires volunteer efforts. People gather supplies for those displaced by conflict. They organize relief teams. They set up shelters or clinics. None of these actions guarantee that violence will never happen again. But they reduce the damage and open paths for reconciliation. They keep hope alive in the middle of turmoil.

Over history, some remarkable individuals have embodied the dream of peace. They were not perfect, but they carried a vision of harmony in their hearts. They spoke of nonviolence and mutual respect. They believed that love could overcome hatred. In their time, many doubted them. They faced ridicule or threats. Yet they continued, guided by a steadfast commitment to peaceful means. Their dedication inspired millions. Over generations, their words and actions still resonate. We see their influence in civil rights movements, humanitarian work, and global peace initiatives. Their legacy proves that dreaming of peace is not a passive act. It is an active choice. It demands moral courage and resilience. It often requires sacrifice. Yet it can unify entire nations. It can transform enemies into allies. It can show us that the human spirit is capable of greatness when it holds onto hope and kindness.

People sometimes ask how they can start dreaming of peace in their own lives. One simple method is to set aside a few minutes each day for reflection. Close your eyes and imagine a peaceful situation. It might be your workplace functioning smoothly. It might be your family sharing laughter without tension. It could be a larger scene of people from different backgrounds celebrating together. Feel the sense of harmony in that imagined moment. Let it fill your mind. Notice any warmth or comfort it brings. Then carry that feeling into your everyday interactions. This practice does not erase problems. But it can shape how you respond to them. Another idea is to engage in peaceful dialogues. Listen sincerely to others, even if you disagree. Look for common values. Show respect. When conflicts arise, find nonviolent ways to resolve them. These steps keep the dream of peace alive in daily life.

Another way to encourage this dream is through creativity. Write about peace in a journal. Paint scenes that reflect unity. Compose music that soothes the spirit. When we create something that reflects our hopes, we strengthen our belief in those hopes. We also share them with others who see or hear our work. We invite them to join us in that vision. This is how dreams spread. This is how they become part of collective action. When enough people share the same dream, they can shift a culture. They can normalize empathy and cooperation. They can counter the messages of division that often flood our media. They can influence decision-makers to invest in programs that heal rather than harm. It all begins with the spark of imagination. By dreaming of peace, we permit ourselves to believe in something better. Then we begin to act on that belief.

The importance of dreaming of peace lies in its transformative power. It affects us from the inside out. It helps us cultivate compassion in our families and communities. It reshapes the way we solve problems and approach disagreements. It influences laws and policies when enough people make their voices heard. It reminds us that we share one planet and one human family. This importance cannot be overstated. Peace is not just the absence of war. It is also the presence of understanding, tolerance, and justice. Dreaming of peace encourages us to build bridges rather than walls. It calls us to be mindful of our words and actions. It challenges us to speak up against injustice. It pushes us to extend a hand of friendship to strangers. It opens our hearts to the notion that every life has value. In this sense, peace is more than a dream. It is a noble pursuit.

Sometimes, people think of peace as boring or static. They assume that if the conflict ends, life loses its excitement. The truth is quite different. A peaceful life can be rich with creativity, diversity, and passion. People are free to express themselves without fear. They can explore art, science, and philosophy. They can exchange ideas without hostility. In such an atmosphere, discoveries thrive. Economies can grow more fairly because resources go toward development rather than destruction. Children can learn without the shadows of violence hanging over them. This is not a fantasy. There are places in the world where, despite challenges, communities live together in relative harmony. They celebrate festivals and share traditions. They benefit from supporting each other's businesses. They protect their environment for future generations. This vision is not perfect, but it shows that peace can be vibrant and dynamic, rather than dull or stagnant.

Yet, peace remains fragile in many parts of the world. Political struggles, resource conflicts, and historical grievances can erupt at any moment. This fragility makes dreaming of peace even more vital. It compels us to keep seeking solutions that avoid violence. It urges us to listen to grievances and find fair resolutions. It reminds us that genuine peace is built on equality and respect. If people feel excluded or oppressed, it undermines stability. Dreaming of peace means addressing these issues head-on. It means acknowledging the mistakes of the past and working to heal old wounds. It means being honest about injustices. It means striving for fairness in our institutions. None of this is simple or quick. But the dream keeps us moving. It helps us persist when the process seems slow. It keeps hope alive, even in places where conflict has raged for decades. That is the power of this vision.

To maintain hope, people often share inspiring stories of reconciliation. They talk about former enemies who now cooperate for the common good. They highlight regions where ceasefires led to dialogue, and dialogue led to cooperation. They celebrate small steps, like a local community center that hosts meetings between different ethnic groups. They note the courage of individuals who refused to return hatred with hatred. These examples show that peaceful outcomes are possible. They are not guaranteed, but they can happen through dedication and empathy. Dreaming of peace allows us to see these moments of success as seeds for a better future. Even a single act of forgiveness can shift an entire narrative. Even one handshake between rival leaders can send a message of possibility. These gestures may seem small, but they hold tremendous symbolic weight. They remind us that peace is a choice we can make, day after day.

We should also remember that peace begins with each of us. It starts with how we treat our neighbors. It grows through our willingness to be patient. It flourishes when we refrain from speaking hurtful words. It blossoms when we do our best to resolve misunderstandings. Even in small daily conflicts, we can practice dreaming of peace. When we face tension at work or home, we can pause. We can recall the vision of a harmonious outcome. We can ask ourselves, "How would I act if I truly believed in peace?" That question can guide us to a kinder response. Over time, these small choices add up. They shape our character and influence those around us. They prove that peace is not only a huge global concept. It is also an intimate part of our personal lives. This dual nature of peace makes it both profound and approachable.

In conclusion, dreaming of peace is a powerful force. It shapes our perspective, influences our behavior, and kindles hope in difficult times. It creates ripples that extend from the individual to the family, community, nation, and the world. Its social impact can be immense, as it fosters cooperation, reduces conflict, and allows societies to flourish. Its importance is evident in every sphere of life, from personal well-being to global diplomacy. There are challenges, including skepticism and adversity, yet those who hold this dream find strength in its vision. This dream is rooted in both ancient wisdom and modern science. It is something we can practice through visualization, dialogue, and everyday acts of kindness. It reveals a path that is neither naive nor easy, but deeply transformative. As we continue this journey to inner peace, we carry with us the faith that our dream of peace can light the way for others.

2. Gratitude's Joy

G ratitude can feel like a gentle breeze that warms the heart. It shows us that goodness exists around us, even when life seems tough. We can wake up in the morning and notice the simple things that make the day better. Maybe it is the sunlight through our window. Maybe it is a kind word from a friend. Often, we forget these moments because we are focused on what is missing. We think about our problems and our worries. We feel the weight of responsibilities. We complain about things that go wrong. But when we pause to notice what we already have, we begin to see life differently. Our minds shift from complaints to appreciation. That shift can brighten our mood. It can also remind us that there is beauty in small details. It can remind us to say thank you to the people who help us.

Gratitude is not about ignoring difficulties. It does not mean that pain disappears. Life can still be hard. We can still face stress at work or tension in relationships. We can still worry about money or health. But gratitude adds a new layer to our experience. It shows us that even in bad times, some blessings remain. We might have a supportive friend who listens. We might have the strength to keep going despite setbacks. We might find unexpected kindness from a stranger. These moments can feel like tiny lights in a dark room. They do not erase the darkness, but they reduce our sense of loneliness or hopelessness. They give us a reason to keep believing in a better future. The act of being thankful can become a source of hope. In that sense, gratitude is a tool for emotional resilience. It offers a fresh perspective when we need it most.

When we practice gratitude, we also connect more deeply with others. People enjoy being appreciated. They feel seen when someone thanks them. They often become more motivated to do good. Gratitude strengthens bonds between friends, colleagues, and family members. It can improve the atmosphere in a group setting. It can build trust. A genuine thank you can defuse tension. It can mend a broken relationship. It can heal old wounds by acknowledging past kindness. It can soften anger by reminding us that the person who upsets us also has positive qualities. This change in our outlook can shift the dynamic between two people. It can also ripple out to affect the larger community. Sometimes, a sincere word of thanks or a small gesture of appreciation can inspire others to show gratitude too. They see it and realize they can do the same. Over time, this creates a culture of kindness that benefits everyone.

Socially, gratitude can have a big impact. Communities that encourage appreciation tend to be more caring. Neighbors look out for one another. Volunteers step up to help those in need. Leaders remember to thank their teams, fostering loyalty and dedication. Schools that teach gratitude to children often see improvements in behavior. Students learn to respect their teachers and each other. They become more willing to share and cooperate. Workplaces that embrace gratitude often report happier employees. These employees feel valued. They feel that their work matters. They are more productive and creative. They become more likely to support their colleagues when challenges arise. By contrast, environments that lack appreciation can breed resentment and negativity. People in such places might feel taken for granted. They might lose motivation and do only the bare minimum. Gratitude is not just a nice extra. It can be a driving force for harmony and productivity.

Gratitude also influences our physical and mental well-being. Research suggests that people who regularly practice gratitude have lower stress levels. They may sleep better. They might have better immune responses. They can handle difficult emotions more effectively. When we focus on what we are thankful for, we release certain chemicals in our brains linked to positive feelings. This helps balance the stress hormones that flood our system when we worry. Over time, being consistently grateful can rewire our thought patterns. Instead of jumping to negative conclusions, we learn to look for the good.

This does not mean ignoring problems. It means facing them with a balanced mindset. Even in times of illness, gratitude can help. It can boost morale and foster hope. It can remind us that life has meaning beyond our current suffering. It can encourage us to cherish the support of friends, family, or caregivers.

Many consider gratitude important because it nurtures humility. When we say thank you, we recognize that we did not do everything by ourselves. We admit that others helped us on our path. We appreciate the sun and rain that allow plants to grow. We honor the efforts of the farmers who picked our fruits and vegetables. We acknowledge the doctors and nurses who treated us when we were sick. We remember the teachers who guided us when we were young. All this is easy to forget in a busy life. We often see ourselves as independent. Yet, in truth, we are linked to countless people we never meet. Every time we buy food or switch on a light, we rely on someone else's hard work. Gratitude reminds us of this network of support. It encourages respect for those who share our world. It makes us less likely to harm or exploit others.

Challenges can arise when we try to make gratitude a regular habit. Sometimes, we might feel that life is unfair. We might face a tragedy that shakes our faith in everything. We might see injustices around us that stir anger. In such moments, gratitude may seem hollow. We might even feel guilty being grateful when others are suffering. We might think that if we focus on blessings, we ignore problems that need attention. But gratitude does not have to silence our compassion or our urge to fix what is wrong. It can exist alongside our activism and our grief. It can keep our hearts open while we fight for change. It can prevent bitterness from consuming us. Another challenge is simply forgetting to be thankful. Our routines can be busy. We run from one task to another. By the time we slow down, we feel exhausted. Yet, with effort, we can weave gratitude into small daily moments.

One lesser-known fact about gratitude is its link to creativity. Some studies suggest that when people feel thankful, they tend to think more broadly. They see possibilities they might have missed. Their mind becomes more flexible and open. They may generate new ideas or solutions more easily. This could be because gratitude reduces stress and boosts positive feelings. Those feelings can free the mind from fear. When we are less scared, we are more likely to take creative risks or explore new approaches. Another intriguing aspect of gratitude is its effect on memories. People who practice regular gratitude journaling often recall positive events more vividly. They also may feel less weighed down by negative past experiences. This can help them build a more resilient outlook on life. It can give them confidence that good things can happen again in the future. That confidence, in turn, supports their emotional health.

It is fascinating to note that many cultures have rituals around giving thanks. Some ancient societies had harvest festivals to celebrate the crops. They offered thanks to the land and the gods for providing food. In modern times, certain nations hold annual days of thanksgiving. Families gather to express their appreciation for one another. Religious traditions often include prayers or ceremonies of thanks. These shared practices remind people that gratitude is not only a personal emotion. It is also a social activity. It connects us to something bigger than ourselves. It highlights our dependence on nature and community. It reminds us that our lives are intertwined. That sense of belonging can be profound. It can lead to a deeper respect for the world around us. It can also combat feelings of isolation because we see that we are part of a larger whole.

Some people find gratitude easier when they keep a simple journal. They might write down three things they are thankful for each day. These can be small. Maybe they enjoyed a warm cup of tea in the morning. Maybe they received a friendly text message. Maybe they saw a cute dog on their walk. The size of the blessing does not matter. What matters is the act of noticing and appreciating. Over time, this ritual can make gratitude more natural. Others prefer to express their thanks verbally. They make it a habit to say thank you to those around them. They send a note or a message to someone who helped them. They look for any chance to recognize kindness in their lives. This can brighten relationships and spark more frequent acts of generosity. The beauty of gratitude is that it does not cost money. It is available to everyone, regardless of background or resources.

It is also worth noting the importance of balance. Gratitude does not mean forcing ourselves to be cheerful all the time. If we feel sad or hurt, we can allow those emotions without shame. We do not have to pretend that everything is wonderful. Gratitude is about noticing goodness where it genuinely exists. It is about remembering that, despite difficulties, there is still something worthy of thanks. We can hold both sadness and gratitude at once. This can be comforting because it acknowledges the complexity of real life. We can feel overwhelmed by burdens, but we can also remember that not all is lost. Some light remains. That knowledge can bring hope during dark times. It reminds us that our story is not finished. There is still room for healing and growth. Gratitude becomes a lantern that helps us find our way through the tunnel of sorrow or despair.

Challenges to gratitude also come from the consumer culture many of us live in. We are bombarded by ads telling us we need more stuff to be happy. We compare ourselves to people who seem to have better cars, bigger houses, or more glamorous lives. We forget to appreciate what we already have. We might feel envy or discontent. Gratitude can counteract this by shifting our focus. It helps us see the true value of what is already in our hands. It shows us that happiness does not always lie in having more. It can be found in a single genuine smile or a simple meal shared with loved ones. It can be found in our ability to breathe and move freely. Once we realize that, the desire for endless accumulation can fade. We begin to realize that real richness comes from relationships and experiences, not just possessions.

Another challenge is dealing with people who do not reciprocate our gratitude. We might say thank you and expect a similar courtesy, but sometimes we receive indifference. This can feel hurtful, especially if we have made a sincere effort. In such cases, gratitude still has its reward. We are improving our emotional landscape by being thankful. We are reminding ourselves that kindness exists. We are reinforcing positive values in our hearts. Whether or not the other person responds in kind, our sense of peace remains. Over time, consistent expressions of gratitude can soften even the hardest hearts. But if that does not happen, our appreciation can still bring us inner happiness. It keeps us from descending into bitterness. It keeps us aligned with the values we cherish. It reminds us that we have chosen a path of acknowledging good rather than focusing on the negative.

Gratitude also ties into the theme of self-love. Often, people only think of gratitude as directed outward. We thank others, the universe, or some higher power. Yet we can also be thankful for the good we have done ourselves. We can appreciate our strengths and achievements. We can thank ourselves for persevering through rough times. This may feel awkward at first, especially if we are used to criticizing ourselves. But honoring our efforts can fuel self-esteem. It can reduce harsh internal judgments. It can motivate us to continue growing. When we are grateful for who we are and what we can do, we develop a healthier relationship with ourselves. This does not mean becoming arrogant. It simply means recognizing that we deserve kindness, just like anyone else. That recognition can be a powerful step toward emotional balance. It allows us to treat ourselves with compassion.

One little-known fact is how gratitude can influence group rituals. Some teams or families start their meetings or gatherings by sharing something they are thankful for. This practice sets a positive tone. It can dissolve tension before serious discussions begin. It can help people remember the common values they share. It also helps each person feel heard and valued. Another interesting aspect is how gratitude can support moral behavior. People who frequently practice gratitude often feel more responsible for their actions. They become aware of how their choices affect others. They may strive to be more honest and fair, knowing that their life is enriched by a community of support. This awareness can lead to a stronger sense of social responsibility. It can encourage volunteer work, charitable giving, or simple acts of kindness.

The importance of gratitude becomes clearer in moments of crisis. When disaster strikes, people sometimes band together and help each other. They offer food, shelter, and comfort. Later, survivors often express deep gratitude for that assistance. This gratitude can bring communities closer. It can lead to lasting friendships. It can help people rebuild their sense of security. Even in grief, gratitude can appear. Someone who loses a loved one might still feel grateful for the years they shared. They might cherish the memories and lessons that person left behind. This does not remove the pain of loss. But it offers a tender recognition of the value that life holds. Gratitude can coexist with sorrow and can soften its sharp edges. It can preserve the loving aspects of a relationship even after it has ended. In this way, gratitude can be a healing force.

Sometimes, we overlook the simplest opportunities for gratitude. We might forget to thank the bus driver who takes us safely to our stop. We might not notice the co-worker who quietly helps us with a project. We might ignore the fact that we can see, hear, or walk without trouble. When we start paying attention, we find endless chances to say thank you. We begin to see how much we receive each day, often without asking. This realization can be humbling and uplifting at the same time. It can shift our attitude from one of entitlement to one of appreciation. That shift can help us become more patient and understanding with others. It can make us more open to new experiences. It can also make us more resilient when life throws obstacles our way. Gratitude nurtures emotional flexibility.

Teachers and parents can play a big role in fostering gratitude in children. They can encourage kids to say thank you and to notice kindness. They can model gratitude themselves. They can praise a child who shows genuine appreciation. Over time, children learn that recognizing others' efforts is an important part of being human. They see that happiness does not only come from taking. It also comes from valuing what one receives. This lesson can shape their future relationships and success. It can help them resist selfish impulses and build healthy connections. It can also protect them from the emptiness of always wanting more. Gratitude reminds them to be content in the moment, while still setting goals for the future. It provides an emotional anchor that can steady them when life feels chaotic.

As we grow older, gratitude can become a constant companion. We might feel it when we see a beautiful sunset. We might feel it when a loved one laughs. We might feel it when our pet greets us at the door. We might feel it when we share a meal with friends. These moments form the tapestry of our lives. Gratitude allows us to savor them, rather than letting them slip by unnoticed. This savoring can increase our overall sense of well-being. It can reduce the sting of regrets about the past. It can lessen anxiety about the future. When we focus on what is right in front of us, we become fully present. That presence can spark joy in the smallest details. It can transform ordinary events into treasured memories. It can remind us that every day holds a gift if we only look for it.

We sometimes wonder how to maintain gratitude in a world filled with conflict and suffering. The news often highlights disasters, crimes, and arguments. It is easy to feel overwhelmed or cynical. Yet gratitude remains possible, even then. It does not mean denying the existence of suffering. It means recognizing the good that survives despite the darkness. It could be a volunteer organization that rescues animals in a flooded region. It could be a teacher who spends extra time helping a struggling student. It could be a neighbor who lends a hand to fix a broken fence. Every day, countless acts of kindness happen all over the world. Gratitude focuses our attention on these acts. It reminds us that hope still lives. It encourages us to join in and do our part. It turns our frustration into motivation to contribute something positive.

In places where gratitude becomes widespread, the social fabric grows stronger. People share resources more willingly. They respect one another's differences more easily. They show patience in traffic or long lines at the store. They support local businesses and attend community events. They greet each other in passing. Over time, small acts of gratitude and kindness can reduce tension and promote unity. This effect is not magic. It arises from the willingness of individuals to practice grateful awareness, day after day. It takes effort because negativity is often more eye-catching. Complaints spread faster than compliments. Yet, if we stick to a path of appreciation, we can inspire others. We can become an example. Our joy can encourage them to see the blessings in their own lives. That is how gratitude grows and spreads.

Experts sometimes suggest combining gratitude with other positive habits. Mindful breathing can help us calm the mind. Once calm, we can reflect on what we are thankful for. This step-by-step approach can deepen the effect of both mindfulness and gratitude. Similarly, sharing gratitude in a group setting can magnify its impact. Hearing what others are thankful for can remind us of blessings we might have overlooked. It can also build a sense of connection, as we realize that many good things touch multiple lives. Gratitude can even work alongside forgiveness. When we are grateful for the lessons learned from a painful incident, we might find it easier to let go of resentment. Gratitude helps us see that pain does not define us. We can grow beyond it. We can transform hardship into wisdom. This transformation is at the heart of many spiritual teachings.

Gratitude matters because it teaches us to value life as it is. It does not wait for perfect conditions to arise. It finds reasons to be thankful amid imperfections. It looks at a half-empty glass and says, "I am glad there is still water in there." It notices the effort someone made, rather than complaining about what they did not do. It sees the light shining through clouds. It does not blind us to reality. It simply highlights hope and positivity. This outlook can lead to a more peaceful inner state. It can help us be kinder to ourselves and others. It can make challenges less frightening and losses less crushing. Gratitude gives us the energy to move forward. It helps us remember that we are loved and supported if only we take the time to see it. That is why gratitude can be a gateway to deeper joy.

When we keep gratitude close to our hearts, we discover that happiness is not about avoiding problems. It is about noticing the good in every chapter of our lives. It is about feeling appreciation for the laughter we share, the lessons we learn, and the moments we survive. It is about cherishing each new day. Over time, this mindset shapes who we are. We become more compassionate. We become more generous. We become more attentive to the gifts around us. And in doing so, we find an inner peace that does not depend on constant success or applause. It arises from within, grounded in the simple act of giving thanks. That is the quiet power of gratitude. It can transform the ordinary into the extraordinary. It can heal our hearts and build stronger communities. It can guide us to see that, despite all pain and struggle, life holds many reasons to be grateful.

3. Hope's Light

Hope can appear like a small flame in the dark. It can spark when everything else seems lost. It can nudge us to keep going when every step feels heavy. Some describe hope as a gentle voice that whispers, "Tomorrow could be better." Others see it as a bright beam that shines through cracks in a wall of despair. Whatever form it takes, hope carries an uplifting energy. It can stir the mind to believe in good outcomes. It can hold us steady when we feel that life has spun out of control. In times of sorrow, hope becomes a source of courage. In times of joy, it can make happiness even richer. Hope's light is subtle yet powerful. It reminds us that no matter how dark the night is, a new dawn waits to break. It helps us believe that we are not alone. It reassures us that our efforts have meaning, even if success is not guaranteed.

Hope has been described in many ways throughout history. Poets sing of it as a bird that perches in the soul. Warriors speak of it as the shield that guards against defeat. Teachers view it as the spark that ignites a student's curiosity. Doctors rely on it to calm a worried patient who waits for healing. In every corner of the world, hope appears as a universal idea. It transcends language. It goes beyond culture or age. It is something that unites us. We all feel the weight of uncertainty at some point, and we all yearn for a glimmer of brightness that cuts through fear. Hope meets that need. It tells us a story of possibilities. It assures us that today's troubles do not have to define tomorrow. This belief can transform how we think, feel, and act. It can inspire a lost person to seek direction once more.

Many people find hope in small details. A friendly smile from a stranger can bring hope during a lonely day. A phone call with good news can spark hope that more good might follow. Even a flower blooming on a cracked sidewalk can remind someone that life pushes through obstacles. These tiny moments often go unnoticed if we are focused on our worries. Yet they can carry a significance that lifts our spirits. They can become signs that something better is on the horizon. Hope does not demand grand gestures. It can grow out of everyday kindness. It can build itself on modest dreams. It can arise when we learn a new skill or receive encouragement. Each act of goodness, each step forward, each gentle word can feed the flame of hope that burns within. That flame may flicker, but as long as it exists, it can guide us.

Hope's light also holds a social impact. When people share hope, communities become stronger. Families pull together when they believe that unity can solve their problems. Neighbors cooperate when they sense that a brighter future is possible for everyone. Organizations rally around hopeful leaders. These leaders inspire team members to keep trying. This group's sense of hope can fuel larger change. It can push scientific research forward. It can drive movements that demand fairness. It can spark creative solutions to long-standing issues. When hope touches a society, people feel less trapped by the status quo. They may challenge outdated practices. They may stand up for those who cannot stand on their own. They may channel energy into making the world a better place. This is why stories of hope often spread. They remind us that even in the face of seemingly impossible odds, progress can happen. Hope offers momentum.

There is also an inner importance to hope. On a personal level, hope can boost our resilience. It provides a mental anchor that keeps us from drifting too far into despair. It prevents negative thoughts from becoming absolute. When we feel beaten down, a dash of hope can bring us back to balance. It can provide just enough light to see a path forward. Without hope, the mind may collapse under stress. Dreams become pointless. Motivation fades. We might stop trying new things or stop taking risks that could lead to growth. Hope protects us from that emptiness. It fuels our willingness to persevere, to attempt, and to learn from our failures. It assures us that even if we fall, standing up still matters. Hope does not guarantee success, but it allows us to keep believing that success could be within reach. That belief can be a powerful driver.

Hope faces many challenges. One challenge is doubt. We doubt ourselves or the people around us. We read discouraging headlines in the news. We see conflicts that seem never-ending. We face injustice that seems immune to reform. Doubt can sap our hope, especially if we experience repeated failures. Another challenge is the fear of disappointment. Hoping for something can make us vulnerable because there is a chance we will not receive it. Some prefer to avoid hope altogether. They assume that if they do not hope, they cannot be let down. But this outlook can lead to a life of constant caution. It might keep us from feeling the true joy that comes with anticipating good outcomes. It might chain us to a life of low risk, where little growth takes place. Still, doubt and fear can be powerful. They can overshadow the spark of hope. This is why it is important to feed hope carefully, like tending a small flame in a windy field.

Another challenge emerges when the world feels especially dark. Events like natural disasters or widespread violence can shake our trust in the future. In those moments, hope may seem naive. People might argue that hope is pointless in the face of real tragedy. They might call it a fantasy that avoids acknowledging harsh reality. Yet hope can be a means of survival in such times. It can help people maintain their moral compass. It can push them to help neighbors or strangers instead of sinking into apathy. It can encourage them to join relief efforts or to rebuild what was destroyed. It can strengthen the spirit so that despair does not take permanent root. Even if the situation remains terrible, hope keeps the soul alive. It preserves a sense of dignity and kindness. It helps communities hold onto the idea that tomorrow can be different. That idea can sustain them through unimaginable stress.

There are lesser-known aspects of hope that are quite fascinating. One interesting fact is how hope affects physical health. Some studies suggest that people who score high on measures of hope tend to have better health outcomes. They might recover faster from surgery or illness. They might stick to treatment plans more reliably. It seems that hope can boost motivation to take care of oneself. Another intriguing discovery is the link between hope and creativity. Hopeful individuals often think more broadly. They see more paths to a solution. They engage with a problem rather than giving up. This wide perspective can spark inventive ideas. Hope might even strengthen social bonds. People are drawn to those who radiate optimism for the future. They want to be part of that energy, to share in the possibility. All these factors point to hope being more than just a wishful thought. It has real, measurable effects on human behavior and well-being.

Hope's importance in daily life can be huge. It keeps us looking forward. It gives us something to strive for. It helps us wake up in the morning with a sense of purpose. Imagine a person who starts a small business in a struggling economy. They pour their savings into it. They work long hours. They face numerous setbacks. Without hope, they might quit at the first serious problem. But hope holds the vision of eventual success. It inspires them to keep trying. It leads them to adapt and refine their strategy. In the end, their business might thrive because they did not give up. On a smaller scale, hope can help us learn a new skill, like playing a musical instrument. We might get frustrated by how slowly we improve. But hope that we can get better urges us to practice more. This repeated effort leads to results. Hope, therefore, plays a key role in personal growth.

For many, hope is also tied to spiritual or religious beliefs. People find comfort in the idea that a higher power has a good plan for them. They trust that good can emerge from bad events. This can bring them peace during crises. Others find hope in philosophy or humanistic ideals. They believe in the innate goodness of people. They trust in human resilience and empathy. They look at how far we have come, despite obstacles, and they see hope for further progress. No matter the source, hope gives a sense that life holds meaning beyond the immediate. It reminds us that even our struggles can shape better days ahead. This sense of meaning can guard us against despair when life feels random or cruel. Hope can act as a bridge between chaos and order, linking the turmoil of now with the promise of a brighter tomorrow.

In society, hope can also trigger collective action. People rally around shared dreams. They work together to achieve an important goal. They develop movements for social change, environmental protection, or scientific breakthroughs. Hope unites them in believing that change is possible. This unity can be incredibly strong. It pushes large groups to volunteer their time and resources. They form alliances, speak out, and demand progress. They persist even when authorities resist. History shows us many examples where a hopeful movement achieved what once seemed impossible. These outcomes often started with a small circle of believers. Their vision spread because it resonated with others who also yearned for better circumstances. Over time, that dream gained momentum, and the impossible became the new reality. Thus, hope can reshape cultures and nations. It can open doors that were once locked. It can shift attitudes, laws, and opportunities. It can show us that what was considered a fantasy can become real.

Still, hope must be balanced with practical steps. Blind hope, without any action, can lead to disappointment. There is a difference between hoping passively and hoping actively. Passive hope waits for miracles. Active hope seeks ways to create them. Passive hope rests on wishes. Active hope invests time and energy in a goal. It sets plans, embraces learning, and adapts to challenges. It accepts that failure may happen but keeps trying anyway. This form of hope is powerful because it gives us agency. It reminds us that we have a role in shaping outcomes. Even if our efforts do not lead to the perfect solution, we often make strides that would not have occurred without hope. We find partial victories or discover new paths that can benefit us. Active hope fosters a spirit of perseverance. It also encourages cooperation, because people see the point of working together on a shared dream.

Some might wonder if hope is a form of denial. They may feel that being too hopeful is unrealistic. They might say, "Life is hard, so accept it." But hope does not require us to ignore hardship. Rather, it invites us to see hardship as part of a larger story that can still have a positive outcome. Hope does not guarantee ease. It just suggests that something good can arise from effort or unexpected sources. It does not deny the existence of pain. It simply refuses to grant pain the final word. This perspective can calm the heart. It can provide a sense of inner peace. That peace does not come from illusion. It comes from the acceptance that we are more than our immediate crisis. We hold within us the seeds of tomorrow's joy. Even if they remain dormant for a while, hope trusts that they can bloom in time.

Sometimes, hope needs renewing. We might face a series of setbacks that extinguish the flame inside us. We might lose a job, a relationship, or a sense of purpose. When that happens, we can look for reminders of hope in our environment. We can talk to someone who overcame a similar struggle. We can read stories of triumph against the odds. We can take small steps toward something that sparks our interest again. We can also practice gratitude. Recognizing small blessings can rekindle hope because it highlights what is still going right. Over time, this practice can build a reservoir of optimism. It can protect us when life feels unkind. Another way to replenish hope is to engage in service to others. Helping someone else can shift our focus away from our troubles. It can open our eyes to the good we can still offer, which can warm our hearts.

Hope's light is also essential in healing. Doctors often see patients who endure long treatments. The hope for recovery or a better quality of life keeps them going. Families who support a loved one through a tough diagnosis rely on hope to stay strong. They hold onto the possibility of healing, or at least improvement. Hope can also aid the healing of emotional wounds. After heartbreak or betrayal, people might feel shattered. They might believe they will never trust again. Yet if even a speck of hope remains, it can guide them toward gradual recovery. They might reach out to friends, try new experiences, or seek professional help. Over time, they discover that life continues and that joy can return. Hope played a large role in keeping them from giving up entirely. It acts as an internal caretaker, reminding us that pain is not infinite.

Hope's power also extends to innovation. Researchers who work for years on an unsolved problem must rely on hope to stay motivated. Inventors who try dozens of prototypes before success are driven by hope. Hope tells them that if they keep going, they might find the breakthrough. These efforts can end up changing entire industries or saving countless lives. From vaccines to new technologies, many discoveries would not have been possible without someone's determination to keep hoping. This is not a blind fantasy. It is a conviction that solutions can exist, even if we have not found them yet. That conviction fuels hard work, collaboration, and creative thinking. It transforms imagination into reality. Along the way, it may breed countless failures but hope absorbs those failures as lessons rather than final verdicts. This process reveals how hope can shape our world in concrete ways.

In relationships, hope can offer forgiveness and second chances. When a friend disappoints us, we might be tempted to close our hearts. But hope can remind us that people can learn and grow. It can prompt us to talk, to try to understand, and to find a way forward. The same applies to family members who argue or drift apart. If hope exists, they can rebuild their bond. They can remember why they cared for each other in the first place. They can trust that tomorrow might bring a chance for reconnection. Similarly, hope can heal tensions in a community. It can spark dialogue between groups who have clashed in the past. It can foster empathy because hope envisions a future where cooperation is possible. This might not happen overnight, but hope keeps the window open. It guards against the finality of hate. In that way, it acts like a gentle peacemaker.

Hope does not always feel like a blazing sun. Sometimes, it is just a tiny glow. Yet even that tiny glow can guide our steps. We do not need enormous optimism to keep moving. We just need enough to see the next possible course of action. Over time, as we gather small victories or glimpses of kindness, that glow can grow brighter. We might start with hope about a single problem. Then we notice other areas in which hope can help us. Little by little, hope becomes a habit. We begin to approach life with an open mind. We see setbacks as hurdles instead of dead ends. We offer encouragement to those who struggle because we remember how hope once helped us. In this way, hope is contagious. One person's belief in a better tomorrow can inspire a whole network of people. It can create a positive cycle that lifts entire circles of friends or communities.

That is why hope's light is so precious. It is never truly owned by just one person. It spreads if we let it. It can spark a sense of purpose in someone who feels lost. It can heal rifts by reminding us of shared goals. It can bridge gaps between cultures, faiths, and ideologies. It can embolden young minds that dare to dream of solutions to current problems. It can protect older generations from cynicism. Every human being has the capacity for hope, even if some have buried it deep. Bringing that hope to the surface can change everything. It can transform bitterness into resolve. It can shift resignation into determination. It can replace cruelty with compassion. This transition does not happen instantly, but once hope ignites, it sets a process in motion. It invites us to imagine what might be possible. Then it encourages us to take steps to make that vision real.

Hope reminds us that every ending can also be a beginning. When we lose a job, we can hope to find a better match for our skills. When a door closes in our faces, we can hope to open another one. When we lose someone we love, we can hope to find a way to honor their memory and move forward. This does not erase grief, but it shows us that our story continues. Hope reassures us that there is more to our journey than the tragedy we have faced. It reminds us that our capacity for love and growth remains. It urges us to keep caring, to keep believing, and to stay ready for new chapters in our lives. Without hope, each disappointment would be the final word. With hope, we see life as an ever-evolving tale. We recognize that what is broken can sometimes be repaired or replaced with something different but meaningful.

On a grand scale, hope can inspire global collaboration. Scientific communities across the world share data with the hope of solving big problems like climate change. Nations with strained relationships still join forces on medical or humanitarian missions. Volunteers travel far to help in areas affected by famine or disasters, fueled by the hope that their efforts can make a difference. Even in war-torn places, some people strive to maintain schools or healthcare facilities. They do so because they have hope that future generations deserve better. Without that hope, such acts of courage and service might never occur. Hope is thus not only about personal growth. It is about collective progress. It is about refusing to accept that the world must remain trapped in its worst patterns. It is a statement that we believe humanity can do better, even if mistakes are repeated. Hope is not blind to flaws. It simply refuses to give up on the possibility of improvement.

We can cultivate hope by directing our attention. If we focus only on negative news, we might drown in despair. But if we look for signs of hope, we can find them. We can read about individuals or groups who are making a positive impact. We can celebrate small successes in our own lives. We can admire acts of kindness that happen every day. By training our minds to notice these hopeful signs, we strengthen our hope. We also become more inclined to create positive actions ourselves. Hope grows when we feed it. We can feed it through gratitude, acknowledging progress, through celebrating each step toward our goals. We can also feed it by surrounding ourselves with people who uplift us. Their encouragement can spark ideas and confidence. In turn, we can uplift others when their hope runs low. That is how hope's light continues to shine and spread.

In the pursuit of inner peace, hope is a key companion. It sustains us through hardships. It reassures us when anxiety creeps in. It urges us to keep a calm heart even in chaos. We know that storms eventually pass, even if we do not know exactly when. Hope assures us that we can find shelter or build it. It tells us that we can work together to survive the worst moments. It reminds us of the inner resilience that humans possess. That reminder soothes the mind and spirit. It helps us endure with grace. It gives us the patience to wait for better days while doing what we can in the present. This sense of possibility can ease tension. It can draw us closer to others. It can reduce the anger and frustration that arise from feeling trapped. It can shift our focus away from panic and toward potential solutions.

Hope's light reveals a path forward. It does not force us to walk that path, but it shows it to us. That is often enough to awaken our willpower. Once we see that a path exists, we might decide to take the first step. We might gather our courage. We might share our hopes with someone else and invite them to join the journey. Along the way, we will meet setbacks. Hope's light might dim at times, but it will not vanish if we continue to feed it. We keep it alive by remembering our past victories. We keep it alive by surrounding ourselves with supportive voices. We keep it alive by focusing on the difference we can make. Step by step, that path can lead us to places we never imagined. And even if the road is tough, we hold onto the knowledge that hope has carried many through tougher roads before.

When we speak of hope, we often invoke images of dawn. The sun rises after a long night, lighting the sky once more. That is the gift of hope: the promise that darkness will break. It is a timeless promise, repeated each day in nature, in our hearts, and in the stories we tell each other. That promise does not ignore that nights can be long. It only states that morning still comes. We hold onto that promise when life tests us. We cling to it when loved ones are in pain. We lean on it when we doubt ourselves. We draw strength from it when we set out on a difficult path. It is hope's steady glow that helps us breathe through fear. It is that same glow that beckons us to try again, to believe, and to strive for better. That is hope's light, shining in every corner of the human experience.

4. Kindness Within

Kindness can appear as a tender touch that eases tension. It can warm a cold heart when no other warmth is there. It often arrives in small acts, like a friendly smile or a comforting word. It shows up when people hold doors open or share a meal with a hungry neighbor. True kindness, however, is not just an outward gesture. It also lives quietly in the mind. It shapes how we see ourselves and others. It motivates us to show compassion, even when no one is watching. It leads us to forgive missteps, both our own and those made by those around us. This inner kindness influences every part of life. It reminds us that our actions carry weight. It tells us we can ease someone's burden, even if we cannot solve all their problems. It whispers that a gentle word can soften the hardest day. It suggests that maybe a grumpy stranger just needs a bit of patience. Sometimes, we forget how powerful a kind deed can be. We might think that kindness is small compared to the world's problems. We might assume that harsher tactics or cold efficiency is the only way to succeed. But deep down, we know that kindness offers a more lasting form of harmony. It nourishes relationships and fosters trust. It helps us see that behind every face is a story that deserves respect. When we embrace kindness within ourselves, we spark a chain reaction that can brighten many lives, including our own.

Kindness carries a social impact that can be surprisingly vast. Communities with a spirit of empathy tend to thrive because people help one another. Neighbors share resources instead of hoarding them. They look out for children and the elderly. They are more likely to volunteer for local projects. This collective kindness creates a sense of belonging. It makes people feel safer and more valued. It reduces stress because individuals know they have someone to lean on. Such communities often see lower crime rates and greater overall happiness. Kindness can also cross cultural boundaries. A caring gesture does not need translation. It can bridge differences in language and background. In a world that sometimes seems split by conflict, kindness remains a universal way to connect. It reminds us that under the surface, we share similar hopes and fears. We yearn for acceptance, security, and love. These shared desires link us, regardless of where we come from. When kindness takes root, it builds a network of support. This network can respond quickly when disaster strikes. It can sustain people when resources are scarce. It can give comfort to those who feel isolated or afraid. Over time, such a culture of kindness can ripple out to impact laws or policies. When enough people value compassion, leaders may prioritize healthcare, education, or aid for vulnerable groups. Society as a whole becomes more balanced because kindness inspires cooperation rather than cutthroat competition. All of this starts with the soft glow of kindness within a single heart.

On a personal level, kindness offers many benefits. It can reduce stress because a kind mind tends to be more forgiving. It does not dwell on grudges for long. It looks for solutions instead of seeking revenge. This approach helps the person practicing kindness remain calm in conflicts. It protects them from the toxic effects of bitterness. It also improves mental well-being. Research often shows that people who engage in regular acts of kindness experience higher levels of satisfaction. They may even enjoy physical health advantages, like lower blood pressure or stronger immune responses. Part of this could be due to the release of certain chemicals in the brain. Doing something good triggers a reward response. The person feels a sense of warmth and connection. This feeling can be addictive in the best way. It leads them to keep seeking opportunities to help. Over time, being kind can become a natural pattern. Even small deeds, like picking up litter in a park, can give a moment of peace. The simple knowledge that one has helped the environment or spared someone else an unpleasant chore can lift the mood. Kindness also boosts self-esteem. When we know we have made a positive difference, even in the slightest way, we feel more valuable. We recognize that our existence can bring benefit to others. This realization often reduces loneliness and despair. It connects us to a sense of purpose that can carry us through tough times.

Kindness does face challenges. A common challenge is a fear of being taken advantage of. Some worry that if they are too kind, others might see them as weak. They might suspect that manipulative people will exploit their generosity. This fear can discourage acts of compassion. Another challenge is time. Modern life can be so busy that people struggle to even take care of themselves. They feel they lack the energy to extend kindness to others. Another obstacle is the mindset that the world is harsh, so we must be harsh too. Some people believe that success only comes from ruthless tactics. They imagine kindness as a distraction from practical realities. They think that if they pause to help someone, they might lose their place in line. They might miss out on opportunities. These pressures make kindness seem impractical. There is also the issue of personal stress. When individuals are overwhelmed, kindness can fade into the background. They might lash out or ignore chances to be compassionate because they have too many burdens themselves. Yet, it is precisely in those moments of stress that kindness can bring relief. When we are kind to others, we often feel better ourselves. When we show compassion for ourselves, we gain the strength to handle setbacks. Kindness can soften anger. It can soothe anxiety. It can mend wounds in relationships that are about to break. However, none of this happens automatically. We must consciously choose kindness, especially when life is tough.

Many interesting facts about kindness are not widely known. One fascinating discovery is the psychological effect known as the "helper's high." When a person does something kind, the brain may release endorphins. These chemicals can create a mild feeling of euphoria, similar to what runners experience. Another fact is how kindness can improve workplace culture. Organizations that encourage employees to be kind often see higher job satisfaction. They observe reduced turnover and increased loyalty. Workers in such environments report feeling that their contributions matter. This sense of belonging sparks creativity. It can boost productivity and inspire teamwork. Also, kindness in schools can enhance learning. When teachers are kind, students feel safer to share ideas and ask questions. They worry less about ridicule, so they explore subjects more freely. This fosters deeper understanding. It also encourages empathy among classmates. Another lesser-known point is the link between kindness and conflict resolution. People who approach disputes with kindness, rather than aggression, often find solutions more quickly. They create an atmosphere where both sides can speak openly without fear. This promotes mutual respect, which is vital for lasting peace. Finally, kindness can protect against depression. Studies suggest that engaging in volunteer work or simple acts of kindness lifts mood over time. It gives people a sense of meaning and breaks the cycle of negative thoughts. All these insights highlight why kindness is more than just a virtue. It is a powerful influence on mental, emotional, and social well-being.

The importance of kindness extends beyond any single moment. It becomes a guiding principle for how we treat ourselves and others. When kindness blossoms within, it shapes our thoughts. It encourages us to interpret events with compassion, instead of suspicion or hostility. This shift can change everything. We might see a rude driver as someone who is overwhelmed, instead of a jerk. We might see a coworker's mistake as an opportunity to offer support, rather than a reason for scorn. We might even see our flaws in a softer light. Instead of berating ourselves for not being perfect, we can practice patience and self-forgiveness. This kindness within lays a foundation for healthier relationships. Friends and family members feel safe to share their worries. Partners are more willing to communicate problems early before they become crises. Children grow up feeling valued. They learn that mistakes are part of growth, not a reason for shame. Over time, this outlook can reduce tension and conflict in the home. It can create an environment where people feel free to learn from errors. On a larger scale, kindness can influence entire communities or institutions. Leaders who practice kind decision-making often earn respect. Their teams trust them because they see genuine care in their actions. This trust leads to more open dialogue, which usually results in better decisions overall. In these ways, kindness becomes a cycle of positivity. It inspires empathy, fosters trust, and guides us toward solutions that benefit many.

Kindness also has a spiritual or philosophical dimension. Many faith traditions teach the value of compassion for all beings. They see kindness as a sacred duty or a path to enlightenment. Humanistic beliefs also celebrate kindness, framing it as a pillar of ethical living. Secular approaches may view kindness as a logical choice since cooperative societies are more likely to survive than hostile ones. Whatever the frame, the core idea is the same. Kindness uplifts life. It resonates with our innate desire to connect and protect. It moves us away from isolation and violence. For those seeking inner peace, kindness can be a guiding light. We discover that peace is not just about personal calm. It also grows when we reduce the suffering around us. Each compassionate act can calm someone's anxiety. It can reduce anger, frustration, or despair. It can prevent harsh words or harmful behaviors. Thus, kindness is deeply tied to the pursuit of peace in both the personal and social arenas. When we practice kindness, we often feel more at ease in our hearts. We sense a harmony between our values and our deeds. That harmony supports emotional balance. It reduces inner conflict. It helps us fall asleep with a lighter conscience, knowing that we tried to do good. This sense of wholeness is precious.

Some people wonder how to cultivate kindness within themselves. One approach is mindfulness. If we slow down and notice our thoughts, we can detect moments when we slip into negativity. We might see ourselves getting irritated at slow internet or a colleague's behavior. By pausing, we can choose a kinder response. Another way is to practice small acts of kindness regularly. This can be as simple as holding open a door, offering a genuine compliment, or helping someone carry groceries. These gestures help kindness become a habit. Over time, they change our perspective. We start looking for opportunities to help, instead of ignoring them. Another method is to reflect on the kindness we have received. We can recall moments when someone forgave us or gave us a chance. We can think about the unconditional support from family or friends. These memories can stir gratitude, which often leads to kindness in return. Also, self-care is crucial. When we are exhausted or overwhelmed, it is harder to be kind to others. So we should allow ourselves moments of rest and self-compassion. We can remind ourselves that kindness is not a one-way street. It should flow both inward and outward. If we neglect our well-being, we might end up resentful or burnt out. Balancing care for ourselves with care for others is key.

There is another important aspect: kindness is not always easy. Sometimes, it may ask us to step out of our comfort zone. We might have to show kindness to someone who hurt us, or to someone we do not understand. We might have to let go of our pride or prejudice. True kindness does not mean pretending we like everything someone does. It means we treat them with respect anyway. We can disagree while still showing empathy. We can call out harmful behavior while still valuing the person behind that behavior. This can be tough, especially when emotions run high. Yet it is precisely this challenge that makes kindness so powerful. It is easy to be kind to those who are kind to us. The real test is extending kindness in less pleasant situations. This does not require being a doormat. Sometimes the kindest act is drawing a boundary or preventing further harm. But we can do so without hatred in our hearts. We can act firmly while preserving the other person's dignity. We can approach conflicts with the aim of healing rather than destroying. This approach might not solve everything. Some problems are deep and require more time. Still, kindness reduces the damage. It encourages resolution rather than fueling the flames of anger.

When we look at history, we see that many leaders who inspired positive change relied heavily on kindness. They believed in the dignity of all humans. They protested injustice, but they also promoted compassion. Their words resonated with millions because they spoke from a place of empathy. They urged people to see one another as brothers and sisters, not as enemies. They exposed cruelty by contrasting it with kindness. That contrast shone a spotlight on how needless many forms of suffering are. Today, their legacies remind us that kind hearts can spark transformations. They show that kindness is not weak. It can move crowds and topple unjust systems. It can bring together former rivals. It can even pave the way for peace treaties or cross-border initiatives. In everyday life, we see smaller but equally meaningful examples. People donate time, money, or skills to help strangers. They set up food banks or tutor programs. They visit the lonely or comfort the sick. These acts might not grab headlines, but they sustain our shared humanity. They keep hope alive in places overshadowed by despair. They show that our instinct is not to tear each other apart but to come together.

Kindness can also open doors to personal growth. When we help someone, we may discover hidden strengths in ourselves. We learn patience, communication, and empathy. We might find that we can handle more responsibility than we expected. We might see that we have talents for organizing, teaching, or healing. This self-discovery can boost our confidence. It can reveal new paths in life. For instance, a student who volunteers at an animal shelter might realize a passion for veterinary work. Or a retiree who mentors young people might decide to become a tutor. Acts of kindness can lead us to unexpected callings. Furthermore, kindness helps us manage anger and frustration. When our focus is on being helpful, we become less likely to lash out. We train ourselves to respond thoughtfully instead of reacting blindly. This not only improves our relationships. It also reduces the internal turmoil that comes from holding grudges. Living with fewer grudges frees up mental space. We can then devote more energy to positive pursuits, creative endeavors, or simple joys. In this sense, kindness is not just about virtue. It is also practical. It paves the way for a more productive and harmonious life.

Often, people assume kindness must be grand to matter. They think they must start a charity or donate large sums of money. While such gestures are wonderful, they are not the only ways to practice kindness. Even the smallest acts can have a ripple effect. A friendly greeting might make someone's day. That person, now feeling positive, might do a favor for a friend. That friend, feeling touched by the gesture, might help another in need. The chain of kindness grows longer with each new link. None of this requires a big budget or a special title. It only needs a willing heart. The result can be a quiet revolution of goodwill. Researchers have found that people who witness acts of kindness also feel inspired. Observing kindness can stir our emotions and nudge us to join in. This is sometimes called "moral elevation." It is a reminder that kindness is contagious. We can spread it simply by being consistent in our thoughtful choices. Over time, our circle of influence can grow, touching people we never meet directly.

Kindness within also shapes how we react to our own mistakes. We often judge ourselves harshly. We scold ourselves for failing or for not living up to expectations. This can create a cycle of shame that paralyzes growth. When we practice self-kindness, we recognize that error is part of being human. We allow ourselves to learn from slip-ups. We treat ourselves with patience and understanding. This self-compassion does not mean letting ourselves off the hook entirely. It means we correct our course without tearing ourselves down. We can admit a mistake, repair any harm caused, and move on with renewed insight. This approach nurtures resilience. It helps us bounce back faster. It also sets an example for how we treat others who err. If we can be gentle with ourselves, we are more likely to be gentle with someone else. This mutual kindness creates a supportive environment. People feel safe to admit they do not have all the answers. They become open to feedback and collaboration. They see mistakes as lessons instead of a source of constant shame.

In many traditions, kindness is seen as a core virtue that can anchor all other positive traits. Patience grows more naturally when grounded in compassion. Honesty becomes gentler and less hurtful when paired with empathy. Courage can be guided by a desire to protect rather than harm. All these traits interlock to create a well-rounded character. Kindness acts as a glue that holds them together in a balanced way. Without kindness, even well-intentioned qualities can turn harsh or harmful. For instance, courage without compassion can become recklessness. Honesty without empathy can become cruelty. In this sense, kindness is a stabilizing force. It aligns our strengths with our moral responsibility to care for one another. It helps us avoid extremes. It also keeps us from losing sight of our shared humanity. No matter how skilled or intelligent we become, kindness reminds us that our ultimate worth lies in how we treat others. It reminds us that every person deserves dignity.

Sometimes, people hesitate to practice kindness because they feel it is wasted on those who will not return it. Yet kindness is not a transaction. We do not have to receive something in return to make kindness valuable. Its worth lies in the act itself. When we are kind, we affirm our principles. We show that we will not be dragged down by negativity. We set an example for those around us. Perhaps they will not respond immediately, but they might remember our kindness later. It could sow a seed that grows much later in unexpected ways. Even if nothing changes outwardly, we grow internally. Each kind of act reinforces our sense of compassion. It strengthens our inner peace by aligning our behavior with our ideals. This helps us sleep better at night, knowing we did our best to bring light to a challenging situation.

If more people adopt this perspective, it can gradually shift social norms. A society that honors kindness over retaliation becomes more united. Its members feel a shared duty to uplift rather than tear down.

It is also valuable to note how kindness can help us handle global challenges. Many of the problems we face, such as climate change or poverty, require cooperation. Kindness fosters cooperation by building trust and goodwill. When leaders show respect to other nations, negotiations go more smoothly. When communities welcome refugees with compassion, it reduces conflict and resentment. When innovators share knowledge openly, breakthroughs happen faster. All these actions hinge on a willingness to be kind. This does not mean ignoring practical complexities. It simply means approaching them with a willingness to understand and collaborate. If we replace fear or greed with mutual care, we stand a better chance of solving large-scale problems. Kindness is not a naive dream. It is a practical approach that can unite diverse groups. It transforms enemies into potential partners. It reduces suspicion and fear, opening space for dialogue. In this sense, kindness is crucial not only at a personal level but also at a global one.

The journey to developing kindness within is continuous. We are human, and we may fail at times. We may act unkindly out of stress or habit. This does not negate all our efforts. Each day is a chance to practice again. We can reflect at the end of the day. We can think about moments we handled well and those we regret. We can plan how to do better next time. Over weeks and months, we might see a shift in our behavior. We might find ourselves being more patient in traffic or more gentle in conversations. We might notice that we judge less harshly. We might also see improvements in how others react to us. They might open up more or reciprocate our kindness. They might be inspired to do the same for someone else. This positive cycle can strengthen bonds we did not even know we were missing. As kindness grows within us, it brings unexpected blessings. We feel calmer and more confident in who we are.

Kindness does not demand perfection. It does not ask us to be saints. It simply nudges us to consider how our actions and words affect others. It asks us to offer help when we can and to refrain from harming if possible. It recognizes that everyone we meet is carrying some secret burden. Even a quick gesture of support can mean a lot. That moment might be the difference between someone losing hope and finding a reason to keep trying. And in giving this support, we also receive. We feel a sense of shared humanity that lifts our souls. This is why kindness within is such a treasure. It changes how we see our neighbors and how we see ourselves. It opens the heart to new connections. It transforms simple routines into chances to spread warmth. It can heal old wounds by focusing on compassion instead of revenge. It can break cycles of hatred by introducing empathy at critical moments. It can help us stand up for justice without losing our gentleness.

When we carry kindness within, we approach life with a softer gaze. We see that every living being is worthy of respect. We recognize that conflict can be eased through understanding. We become more adept at settling disputes because we seek resolutions that respect all sides. We also become gentler in judging ourselves. We accept that we are a work in progress. This acceptance frees us to keep evolving. We realize that every day holds a chance to act kindly in a new way. Whether we succeed or stumble, we try again tomorrow. In the larger scheme, these individual efforts weave together to form a community of caring. They form neighborhoods where people look out for one another. They form workplaces where empathy guides decisions. They shape a world where help can arrive before hate. They remind us that we can choose compassion over indifference. Even when the world seems chaotic, this choice remains ours to make. We can embrace kindness as our inner compass, guiding each step. In doing so, we carry a piece of peace wherever we go. We stand as a beacon to those who have lost faith in the goodness of others. We show that kindness has not vanished. It is still here, alive in each small moment of caring, waiting to grow. In that growth lies the path to a gentler future for all.

5. Boundless Love

Boundless love can feel like a soft embrace that wraps around every part of our being. It can fill the mind with warmth that seems to have no end. It can reach across miles and include strangers we have never met. It can break down the barriers we erect out of fear or habit. This type of love is not confined to romance or family ties alone. It stretches far beyond the usual definitions. It can extend to neighbors, coworkers, and entire communities. It can rise from deep within us and flow outward without limits. The idea of boundless love has existed in various cultures for centuries. Yet, we often forget how powerful this force can be when truly unleashed. We may hear about it in poetry or songs, but rarely do we pause to feel its full potential. When we allow it to blossom, it can uplift us and those around us in countless ways.

Boundless love does not require everyone to be perfect. It does not hide from flaws or disagreements. Instead, it invites us to see beyond those surface issues. It reminds us that every person holds a spark of worthiness. This broad viewpoint can transform our daily interactions. Where we used to see a rude comment, we might now see a wounded soul reaching out for help. Where we used to feel threatened, we might now sense an opportunity to understand. This does not mean we excuse harmful actions. Rather, we hold the conviction that every being is worthy of respect. We choose to see the potential for better behavior, even when it is not obvious. This shift in perspective can lighten our burden. It can free us from the desire for revenge or from the obsession with grudges. It can help us move through the world with more patience.

Boundless love also affects our sense of self. When we offer love without strict conditions, we often find it easier to love and accept ourselves. We see that we, too, make mistakes but remain deserving of compassion. This self-compassion nurtures inner peace. It reduces the harsh self-criticism that can plague our thoughts. It reminds us that if we extend boundless love to others, we should not exclude ourselves from that circle. In turn, this acceptance can foster healthier habits. We might take better care of our bodies, our minds, and our spirits. We might let go of toxic shame or perfectionism. We might also become more open to personal growth, recognizing that mistakes are part of learning rather than signs of worthlessness. This view builds a gentle foundation upon which we can stand more confidently in life. It gives us room to breathe, to evolve, and to offer more kindness to the world around us.

A society that values boundless love can experience profound benefits. People are more inclined to cooperate when they feel valued for who they are. Communication tends to be clearer because there is less fear of judgment. Shared goals become more achievable. Schools that champion the idea of loving respect see students who are kinder to one another. Bullying often decreases. Empathy rises. Children learn early that everyone deserves care, no matter their differences. Workplaces also gain from this atmosphere. Employees who feel genuinely seen and appreciated are more likely to stay motivated. They collaborate more willingly and support one another in projects. This fosters innovation. It saves organizations from endless conflicts and resignations. On a broader scale, entire communities can unite around the common good. They can build strong networks of mutual support. They can develop programs for the poor or neglected members. They can invest in future generations with a spirit of genuine concern. These actions can reshape the way a nation or culture operates, guiding it toward unity rather than constant division.

The importance of boundless love becomes particularly clear in times of crisis. When floods, earthquakes, or other disasters strike, people often come together in remarkable ways. Volunteers travel from distant places. Neighbors share supplies. Strangers risk their lives to save each other. This happens because, for a moment, we remember that we are all connected. We see that our differences matter less than our shared humanity. In these times, boundless love emerges as the force that allows us to endure tragedy and recover. It can give hope to those who have lost everything. It can make the rebuilding process more efficient, as people pool their talents and resources. Over and over, we see that crises bring out the best in many. The challenge is learning to sustain this boundless love long after the immediate disaster ends. If we can maintain that sense of unity, we might prevent future catastrophes from being so devastating. We might address the social and environmental issues that worsen these events. We might also heal old wounds that fester during peaceful periods, eventually causing deeper conflicts.

There are many challenges to embracing boundless love. One common obstacle is fear. We fear being hurt if we open our hearts without reservation. We worry that our kindness may be exploited. We suspect that people might not return our love. These concerns are not baseless. Vulnerability can bring pain. Another challenge is distrust fueled by past experiences. Perhaps we have faced betrayal or rejection. The memory of that pain can cause us to shield ourselves. We build walls to keep others from coming too close. We act tough or distant, afraid to be seen as weak. In doing so, we might block ourselves from the joy that genuine connection can bring. Another obstacle is societal conditioning that promotes competition or suspicion. Many are taught that life is a battle for limited resources. This mindset makes boundless love appear naive. People might say, "Real life doesn't work that way." Yet, when we look deeper, we see that collaboration and empathy often lead to better outcomes for everyone. The real challenge is balancing prudent caution with open-hearted care. We do not need to discard common sense. Instead, we can hold an underlying belief in the value of each being while also setting healthy boundaries. This approach allows us to remain loving without becoming a doormat. It is a skill that requires practice and self-awareness. Over time, we can refine it.

A lesser-known aspect of boundless love is how it influences the brain. Studies hint that engaging in loving thoughts or loving-kindness meditations can alter certain neural pathways. These changes may reduce stress and increase a sense of well-being. They can even enhance empathy. Another surprising fact is how widespread the concept of boundless love is in different spiritual and philosophical traditions. Ancient teachings often encourage love for all creatures, not just humans. They speak of the importance of extending care to animals, the planet, and future generations. Modern psychology echoes this, noting that a sense of global empathy can improve our overall mental health. Science also reveals that acts of caring release beneficial chemicals in the body. These chemicals can lower blood pressure and strengthen the immune system. Even small acts, like comforting a friend, can bring these effects. This suggests that boundless love is not only beneficial in a moral sense. It also has tangible physical benefits for those who practice it.

The idea of boundless love also holds importance in personal healing. People who have been hurt or who struggle with trauma sometimes find solace in loving others or engaging in altruistic acts. Helping another can restore a sense of purpose. It can help them see that they are not defined by their pain. Instead, they can channel their experiences to empathize more deeply. When this process is guided by professionals or by supportive friends, it can lead to substantial emotional growth. Boundless love, therefore, can serve as a powerful tool in therapy and recovery. It shifts focus away from the self as a broken entity. It highlights the potential for connection and contribution. It says, "Yes, I have suffered, but I can still offer love." That realization can be transformative. It can break chains of anger or bitterness. It can replace despair with a sense of meaning. It reminds us that in giving love, we often receive emotional nourishment in return.

Families can also reap benefits from boundless love. Parents who show unconditional care to their children help those children develop healthy attachment patterns. This does not mean giving them everything they want. It means consistently affirming that they are loved, even when their behavior requires correction. Children raised in this environment often become more secure adults. They learn to handle conflict without feeling they must defend their worth. They also pick up on the model of loving behavior and carry it forward in their relationships. Partners who practice boundless love with each other can weather misunderstandings more easily. They approach disagreements with a desire to reconcile rather than to win. They work together to find solutions that respect both parties' needs. Over time, this creates a foundation of trust and mutual support. Extended families that foster this outlook can reduce long-standing feuds. They can help the younger generation understand the value of unity. Boundless love becomes the thread that keeps the family fabric strong, even if individual members have significant differences.

Some might wonder if boundless love is realistic. They might say that hatred, greed, and conflict are just part of human nature. Such negative forces indeed exist. However, love also exists as part of human nature. We see it in the countless everyday acts of kindness that go unreported. We see it in strangers who step in to help a person who has fallen in the street. We see it in volunteers who give up free time to serve in shelters or community centers. Boundless love does not demand that we close our eyes to evil. Rather, it stands as a steadfast commitment to good despite evil. It says, "I acknowledge darkness exists, yet I choose to shine a light." That light can take many forms. It might be a simple smile or a phone call to someone who feels alone. It might be an effort to mediate between two people locked in anger. It might be advocacy for those who cannot speak for themselves. Each form reflects the same core principle: we do not give up on compassion, no matter how bleak things appear.

Sometimes, people worry that showing boundless love will leave them with nothing. They fear it implies endless giving until they are drained. Yet true boundless love, as taught by wise figures throughout history, starts with recognizing our worth. We cannot truly give what we do not allow ourselves. If we want to offer unwavering compassion, we must learn to be compassionate with our own needs and limits. This means taking time to rest, seeking support when we need it, and respecting our well-being. Boundless love is not about self-sacrifice that leads to burnout. It is about cultivating a well of empathy that can keep flowing without leaving us empty. That well is replenished by self-care, nourishing friendships, and honest communication about what we can and cannot do. This healthy approach lets us love without fear. We know we are not forced to destroy ourselves in the process.

Another point about boundless love is how it enables forgiveness. Forgiveness does not excuse wrongdoing. Instead, it releases the hold that resentment can have on our hearts. When we love in a boundless way, we understand that clinging to anger hurts us as much as, or more than, the other person. We may still set boundaries to protect ourselves from further harm. But we free ourselves from the heavy chain of hate or bitterness. This act can be life-changing. It allows us to move forward rather than remain stuck in the past. It also opens the door to potential reconciliation if the other party shows true remorse. Even if reconciliation never happens, forgiveness allows us to find emotional freedom. This freedom can spark creativity, healing, and joy that were once locked away. In many traditions, forgiveness stands as a central pillar of love, because it cleanses the heart of negative energy.

Boundless love also helps in bridging social divides. Humans have a habit of forming in-groups and out-groups. We bond with those we see as similar, and we may distrust those who seem different. Boundless love questions this habit. It invites us to see people from different backgrounds, races, or beliefs as part of the same human family. It challenges the idea that we must compete or despise each other. In a polarized world, this perspective can feel radical. Yet, it often leads to unexpected friendships. It can also reduce conflicts, as empathy replaces knee-jerk hostility. Over time, if enough people practice this form of love, entire communities can become more inclusive. This does not mean ignoring real issues or disagreements. It means addressing them with an outlook that values dialogue and respect. This approach can soften tensions and open spaces for compromise. It can pave the way for policies that protect minority groups. It can encourage the sharing of resources in fairways. Thus, boundless love has the power to reshape social structures from the grassroots up.

Many find that art captures the spirit of boundless love. Whether it is a painting, a song, or a poem, artistic expressions of love can stir the heart. They remind us that we are all searching for belonging and acceptance. Stories of heroic acts fueled by love become timeless because they reflect a deep human truth. People resonate with tales of someone who risks everything for the sake of compassion. Such narratives can inspire us to look for that same courage within ourselves. Even watching a film about selfless love can bring tears to our eyes. Those tears often come from recognizing that we too yearn for that level of care. We, too, have a spark of it inside us. It is a shared human longing that art captures so vividly. When we embrace this longing and turn it into action, we begin to see love as a daily practice, not just an ideal.

Boundless love can also enhance our relationship with nature. Some traditions speak of loving the Earth as part of loving all beings. They urge us to protect forests, oceans, and wildlife out of respect for the unity of life. Modern science shows that the health of the planet is linked to our health. If we pollute the environment, we harm ourselves. Boundless love reminds us that we do not stand separate from the rest of nature. We are deeply intertwined with ecosystems and other creatures. Caring for them is not a charity act; it is a shared responsibility that secures our common future. By seeing ourselves as part of a larger whole, we make choices that sustain life rather than destroy it. We reduce waste and seek cleaner energy sources. We rethink our consumer habits. These steps reflect a love that transcends borders, species, and immediate self-interest. This is how boundless love can guide us toward environmental stewardship.

At times, people mention the idea of universal love in religious or spiritual contexts. They recall figures like saints or prophets who displayed immense compassion for humanity. Yet this ideal is not reserved for spiritual heroes alone. We can all tap into it. We do not need to perform miracles to show boundless love. We can start with small gestures, building them into a lifelong habit. Over time, these acts might accumulate into a powerful force. They might influence our families, our communities, or even our workplaces. In an age of digital connectivity, even a sincere online message of comfort can reach someone miles away who feels isolated. Each of us can choose to be a small but significant vessel of boundless love. We might not see all the results directly, but the ripple effect can be vast.

Boundless love can also serve as a safeguard against cynicism. When we are bombarded with negative news, it is easy to grow jaded. We might think there is no point in caring because the world seems so broken. But boundless love insists that goodness still exists, often in corners we seldom hear about. It invites us to contribute our goodness rather than withdraw into despair. Each moment of giving or forgiving stands as proof that hope remains. Even if we cannot fix every problem, we can alleviate suffering in our sphere of influence. This refusal to succumb to cynicism nourishes resilience. It lets us stand strong in times of turmoil. It keeps the flame of possibility alive in our hearts. Others may see that flame and rekindle their hope.

On a personal journey to inner peace, boundless love can be a guiding star. It aligns closely with values like compassion, gratitude, and hope. Each of these qualities supports and reinforces the others. When we love widely, we also tend to feel thankful for the people in our lives. We appreciate the lessons each encounter brings. We maintain hope in the face of challenges, trusting that love can outlast any struggle.

This synergy of virtues helps us remain centered. It protects us from becoming too bitter or rigid. It encourages us to meet life's uncertainties with grace. That grace, in turn, supports emotional and mental stability. We find it easier to breathe through conflicts or heartbreak. We recover from setbacks because love remains the bedrock under our feet. In times of triumph, we do not become arrogant, because we remember that everyone deserves a share of joy. Thus, boundless love not only binds us to others, it also binds us to our best selves.

Some may say that boundless love is an impossible dream. They point to endless wars, betrayals, and cruelty in the world. They claim that humans are doomed to fight each other. Yet history also records eras of harmony and examples of reconciliation. It documents times when communities overcame deep grudges to work together. It reveals that change happens when enough people choose empathy over animosity. Boundless love does not demand that we ignore facts or sugarcoat reality. It simply offers a different path. It calls us to focus on what can be built instead of what is broken. It reminds us that the potential for good can rise anew, even from the ashes of destruction. When we adopt that stance, we stand a chance at healing and progress. We take part in the grand human story of finding light despite darkness.

Individuals who practice boundless love often report a sense of freedom. They feel less enslaved by anger or envy. They realize that love is an expansive resource, not limited to a few recipients. They can give affection to their close circle while still caring deeply about the wider world. This attitude fosters a broader sense of responsibility. They see that their actions, no matter how small, contribute to the overall tapestry of life. That knowledge can be both humbling and empowering. It humbles us because we see that we are just one thread among many. It empowers us because we realize that every thread matters. Together, these threads can form a beautiful design if guided by compassion. If we remain too caught up in fear, we might tangle the threads or let them fray. Boundless love helps us keep them woven in unity.

We can nurture boundless love through daily intentions. We can wake up each morning and set the goal to be kinder, to judge less, and to help where we can. We might take a moment to imagine sending love to those who suffer. We can also practice being fully present in our interactions and listening without planning our response. This deep listening can open our eyes to the struggles and dreams of others. It can dissolve misconceptions. Simple exercises like these build the foundation of a loving worldview. Over days and weeks, we notice changes in how we feel and behave. We might find ourselves more patient in traffic or more gentle in disagreements. We might seek out ways to support local causes. We might treat ourselves with less harshness. Slowly, boundless love becomes a more natural response.

Another way to cultivate this love is by learning about different cultures and histories. We discover that every community has heroes, tragedies, and hopes. This learning can dissolve stereotypes and awaken empathy for those who seem different. We see that parents everywhere want the best for their children. We see that each region has unique struggles, but also unique strengths. By expanding our knowledge, we expand our capacity for compassion. We become less trapped by narrow viewpoints that label entire groups as enemies. This mental shift can change how we vote, how we spend money, and how we interact online. It guides us to seek common ground rather than constant conflict. Boundless love grows when we appreciate the interconnected nature of life. We realize that harm done to one group can echo and eventually affect us all.

Boundless love also gives us the courage to confront injustice. It does not mean being passive in the face of wrongdoing. Instead, it means standing up for what is right without fueling hatred. We denounce abuse because we love the victims and also believe in the moral potential of the abusers. We hope they can change, given proper accountability and guidance. This mindset can transform activism into a healing force. It calls for reparation and change, but not for blind vengeance. That approach can lessen the cycle of violence that arises when anger meets anger. It leaves room for dialogue and potential redemption. This does not guarantee success every time. Some conflicts are deep, and some individuals reject any offer of peace. Yet, boundless love urges us to keep the door open. It reminds us that reconciliation is possible, even if rare.

In a fast-changing world, boundless love can help us adapt. Technology brings us into contact with people we might never meet otherwise. It also floods us with news of tragedies far away. Sometimes we feel overwhelmed by the problems we cannot fix. Boundless love helps us process these emotions without turning numb. It encourages us to do our part locally or digitally. It invites us to join global initiatives, if we can, or to at least support them. We learn that we are not powerless. Each small action, each donation, and each message of support can make a difference to someone, somewhere. This sense of shared humanity can reduce isolation and despair. It can give us new connections and new perspectives. It can remind us that, as technology weaves the world together, our hearts can also be woven into a larger collective of caring souls.

In the end, boundless love is more than a lofty idea. It is a path we can choose daily. It starts in small ways: showing patience, offering help, or extending forgiveness. It grows as we practice empathy with people near and far. It shines brightest when we realize it is not limited by borders or boundaries. Love can reach across differences of culture, language, and belief. It finds its place in big gestures and tiny everyday acts. Each time we choose love over fear, we strengthen the bond that holds us all. Over time, those choices can reshape families, communities, and maybe even entire nations. They can bring healing where harm once ruled. They can open hearts that were sealed by pain.

They can create a ripple effect of kindness that extends far beyond our sight. This is how boundless love nourishes the journey to inner peace. It connects the personal quest for harmony with the collective well-being of all. It shows us that our serenity and the healing of the wider world go hand in hand. We see that love's true power is revealed when we do not confine it. We let it flow, trusting that, in the end, what we give returns in some form, or simply brightens a corner of existence we have yet to see. We carry this knowledge forward as we continue on the path, step by step, guided by the infinite light of love that knows no boundary.

6. Strength in Patience

Patience can feel like a soft breeze in a storm. It steadies the mind when chaos grows too loud. It reminds us that progress does not always come at once. It encourages us to wait for the right moment and to trust in a future outcome. Many people see patience as a minor virtue. They think of it as just enduring a situation without losing one's temper. But true patience goes much deeper. It is not about merely putting up with delays or discomfort. It is about finding composure in the middle of stress. It is about learning how to respond instead of react. It is about seeing the long path instead of demanding instant results. When we practice patience, we choose to resist the impulse to force or rush. We decide to stay calm, even if everything around us feels urgent. We discover that this calmness can bring more strength than we ever expected.

Patience has wide-reaching social effects. In families, patience can soothe tense moments before they erupt into quarrels. It can bring people together because a patient person is often better at listening. They let others speak without interruption. They show respect by waiting until someone else finishes their thought. This creates an atmosphere of understanding. It allows everyone to feel heard. Over time, it shapes a more harmonious household. In the wider community, patience fosters cooperation. Patient people tend to avoid heated outbursts in public. They stand in lines without pushing or complaining. They drive with more care and fewer fits of road rage. These might sound like small things. Yet they add up over time. Patience in many individuals can transform a neighborhood, a city, or even a society. It can reduce tension among strangers. It can show children that waiting is normal. A community that values patience often sees fewer conflicts. People let each other merge in traffic. They hold doors open. They wait their turn. The result is a kinder, more polite environment. This might seem simple, but the cumulative effect is significant. It sets a tone of respect. It makes daily life smoother. And it makes big decisions easier to handle together.

Patience also serves a crucial role in personal development. Many goals require consistent effort over a long period. It might be learning a musical instrument or building a business. It could be working through a college degree or practicing a new language. Without patience, we might quit the moment our progress slows. We might get frustrated when we do not see instant results. Patience gives us the grit to continue. It reminds us that mastery does not happen overnight. It tells us that any meaningful skill or project takes time. Even in areas like physical fitness, patience is key. We might exercise for weeks without seeing dramatic changes. But day by day, our body grows stronger. If we abandon our routine too early, we never reach the reward. Patience keeps us on the path. It prevents us from being fooled by quick fixes or false promises. It teaches us that real growth often unfolds in small steps.

Patience also shapes our emotional life. When we are impatient, we tend to snap at others. We feel tension in our bodies. Our minds race with annoyance. This stress can harm our health. Our blood pressure might rise. Our sleep might suffer. We might feel constant anxiety because we want everything done right now. Patience calms these storms. It allows us to breathe. It shows us that not every situation demands immediate action. Sometimes, simply waiting and observing can solve more problems than rushing in. This sense of calm can spread to the people around us. They sense our steadiness and feel safer. Relationships benefit greatly from patience. Friendships deepen when we accept that everyone has flaws. Marriage thrives when partners give each other room to grow. Parents who practice patience with their children teach them valuable lessons. They show that mistakes are part of learning, not reasons to lose one's temper. These children often become more confident. They know they can make errors without being harshly judged. Over time, that attitude helps them develop resilience. It helps them approach challenges with steady determination.

On a broader level, patience can affect how we handle global issues. Many social and environmental problems do not have instant solutions. They call for long-term strategies. Impatience might lead people to think these issues are hopeless. Patience, however, reminds us that real change takes sustained effort. It helps activists continue their campaigns over years or even decades. It keeps scientists committed to research that may not bear fruit for a long time. It can unite communities that need to rebuild after disasters. Patience also plays a role in politics and diplomacy. Negotiations can take a great deal of time. Various interests must be heard. Quick, poorly crafted deals can fall apart. Patient dialogue can lead to more lasting peace or more stable agreements. This does not mean we stop caring about urgent problems. It only means we approach them with a plan that allows for gradual progress. That approach often avoids the pitfalls of hasty decisions. It sets a foundation that can hold up over time, even in the face of new challenges.

There is a special kind of strength hidden in patience. People sometimes see patience as passive, as though you are simply doing nothing. But patience often requires immense self-control. It demands that we resist our impulses to lash out or to quit. It calls on us to remain alert while we wait. This alert waiting is not inaction. It is an active state of readiness. Think of a farmer who sows seeds. They do not keep digging them up each day to check if they have sprouted. They wait with calm faith, tending the soil, and making sure the plants get water and light. That waiting is not laziness. It is a patient's trust in the natural process of growth. Likewise, a parent teaching a child to tie their shoelaces must watch them struggle for a while. They allow the child to figure it out, stepping in gently only when truly needed. The parent stays calm as the child fumbles and tries again. That calm is a form of love. It fosters real learning. It teaches the child to persist. This is the essence of patience as an active presence.

Patience faces many obstacles in modern life. Technology offers fast results with a few clicks. We can order food for delivery in minutes. We can stream entire shows without waiting a week for the next episode. So we grow used to immediate gratification. When something requires extra time, we grow restless. We wonder why it cannot be faster. We might lose respect for the effort behind the scenes. This can weaken our ability to endure slower processes. Another challenge is the pressure to keep up with everyone else. We see people posting achievements on social media. They show off quick successes or glamorous lifestyles. We compare ourselves and feel frustrated. We wonder why we are not at the same level right away. Impatience grows. We push ourselves too hard. We might even cut corners or make poor decisions. This can lead to burnout or shallow results. A further obstacle is fear of missing out. We think if we wait or proceed slowly, we might miss an opportunity. Yet, in reality, being patient can open the door to better decisions. It can allow us to gather crucial information or develop our skills to a higher level. It can keep us from regrets later on.

Patience also shows up in how we treat ourselves. Often, we are impatient with our own emotions. We expect ourselves to get over sadness or anger quickly. We feel that we should be "fine" right away. This can lead to denial or repression of genuine feelings. But emotional healing takes time. We might need days, weeks, or even years to fully process a major life change. By rushing that process, we risk leaving emotional wounds unhealed. True patience with ourselves involves acknowledging that we are on a journey. We cannot skip certain steps. We need to learn from them. This self-patience does not mean wallowing in misery. It means accepting that some inner work cannot be rushed. It means offering ourselves kindness instead of scolding ourselves for not moving faster. Over time, this approach brings deeper healing. It also helps us become more empathetic toward others. If we have tasted the importance of patience in our struggles, we are more likely to grant it to someone else.

Lesser-known facts about patience include findings in psychology. Research suggests that people who practice patience regularly tend to have better mental health. They show lower levels of depression and anxiety. They often feel more satisfied with life overall. Another study links patience to stronger relationships. Patient individuals are more likely to handle conflicts constructively. They listen longer. They respond calmly. They do not rush to anger or rash judgments. Another intriguing discovery is how patience can boost physical health. Chronic impatience often leads to stress-related issues like headaches or weakened immunity. Patience supports better stress management, which in turn can help the body stay healthier. These findings reflect a deeper truth. The mind and body are intertwined. Emotional states can shape physical well-being. Choosing patience helps both mind and body to remain stable and resilient.

Patience also makes a difference in creative work. Artists, writers, and musicians often speak of the need for patience when creating something new. They might spend months revising a piece. They might wait for a spark of insight before adding the final touches. Impatient creators might rush through the process, producing something half-formed. The difference can be felt in the result. Similarly, in scientific fields, breakthroughs require patient research. Scientists test hypotheses again and again. They fail many times before finding a valid solution. Without patience, such discoveries might never happen. Entrepreneurs, too, need patience to build businesses that last. They must refine their product, learn about the market, and earn the trust of customers. Quick profits might tempt them, but the real strength often lies in long-term growth. Patience allows them to adapt and evolve sustainably.

Patience does not mean staying in a harmful situation forever. It is important to distinguish between patience and passive submission.

If someone is in an abusive environment, leaving might be the wisest choice. Patience in that context might mean holding onto hope for one's future while planning a safe exit. It does not mean accepting mistreatment without end. Patience is also different from complacency. We can remain patient with a slow process while still taking steps to move forward. We do not just sit and do nothing, hoping everything will fix itself. We do what we can in each moment. Then we let time handle the rest. This balance can be tricky. We must learn when to wait and when to act. We must see if the moment calls for calm observation or decisive movement. Over time, we develop a kind of wisdom that guides us. We learn to sense the difference between a situation that needs more time and one that requires a direct decision.

The social importance of patience can be seen in conflict resolution. Many disputes escalate because people are quick to speak and slow to listen. They do not wait to hear the full story. They jump to conclusions. They interrupt with their demands. Patience in a negotiation setting can transform the outcome. A patient mediator waits for both sides to air their concerns. They encourage each person to articulate their viewpoint fully. This approach can uncover hidden issues or misunderstandings. It can allow for more meaningful compromise. Patience also appears in healing old wounds between communities. Some historical grudges run very deep. A single conversation will not erase them. But patient and consistent dialogue, over time, can reduce suspicion. It can build trust one small interaction at a time. This process demands endurance. It demands a willingness to see the larger picture instead of immediate gratification. Such patience can lead to lasting peace where quick fixes would have failed.

The strength of patience also plays a part in how we relate to technology. Social media thrives on instant reactions. News headlines urge rapid responses. In this environment, patience might feel outdated. Yet, it is more vital than ever. Without it, we risk spreading misinformation or engaging in unnecessary fights. If we wait a moment, we might discover that an article was misleading. We might learn that a shocking claim was false. Or we might read a bit deeper and see that the situation is more complex than it seemed. Patience online can save us from embarrassment or regret. It can keep us from damaging relationships over misunderstandings. It can guide us to use technology responsibly and not let it dictate our every move. We can wait before posting a heated comment. We can hold off on sharing a rumor. That small gap of time might be enough to prevent a big mistake.

On a personal spiritual or philosophical path, patience serves as a core virtue in many traditions. It is linked to humility because waiting often reminds us that we are not in total control. It is connected to compassion because being patient with someone else's struggles requires empathy. Many meditation practices emphasize patience. They teach us to observe our thoughts and feelings without rushing to change them. This can reveal hidden patterns in the mind. Over time, it can free us from automatic reactions. We learn to pause, breathe, and decide how to respond. That pause is the essence of patience. It is a gap where wisdom can enter. In certain faiths, patience is praised as a step toward enlightenment or holiness. It reflects a willingness to accept life's rhythms and trust in a greater flow. Whether one is religious or not, there is great beauty in embracing patience as a guiding principle. It encourages gentleness in our approach to life. It helps us see that seeds take time to grow, that healing follows its timeline, and that not every dream must materialize this very second.

Patience can also play a direct role in mental discipline. In some studies of willpower, people who show the ability to wait for a reward tend to do better in many life aspects. This is sometimes called delayed gratification. Famous experiments with children and marshmallows tested whether they could wait a few more minutes for a bigger reward instead of taking a small reward right now. Many who waited went on to show higher achievements in later years. That experiment, while simple, points to a deeper principle. Being able to endure short-term discomfort or inconvenience for long-term gain can shape our future success. Patience becomes the key to opening doors that require perseverance. It teaches the mind to hold out for something of greater value rather than grabbing a lesser prize immediately. That lesson applies to finances, careers, relationships, and even health. Saving money demands patience. Investing in one's education demands patience. Building trust in a friendship demands patience. There are no shortcuts that can fully replace the power of slow and steady effort.

Sometimes, patience can feel lonely or misunderstood. When we choose patience, people around us might say we are weak or indecisive. They might push us to hurry up or to demand instant results. We might feel pressured to act against our better judgment. This is where the inner strength truly shines. Patience, rooted in clarity, does not bow to peer pressure. It holds firm when it sees that waiting is the best course. It does not waver just because others fail to see its value. This can be challenging. It might test our courage. But if we stick to it, we often see that our patience pays off. The rushed decisions of others can lead to problems. Meanwhile, our patient approach might bear stable fruit. We then confirm that patience is not about being soft. It is about having the backbone to walk at a different pace, even when the crowd runs in the opposite direction.

In relationships, patience can heal wounds that otherwise might never mend. A friend who is going through a hard time may need more than a quick pep talk. They might need someone who listens day after day. They might take months or years to heal from a deep loss. Being that patient
presence can mean everything to them. It shows they are not alone. It shows that they do not have to recover on anyone else's schedule. Over time, that bond can grow stronger than ever. The same is true in romantic or family relationships. If we demand that our loved ones change immediately, we often face disappointment. We might push

them away. But if we encourage them gently, while giving space for their process, real transformation can occur. They feel our support instead of our pressure. They sense acceptance instead of a rigid demand. This invites them to explore their path with less fear. That exploration can lead to genuine growth. It also deepens mutual understanding, because we learn to see life from their viewpoint.

Patience does not rule out setting goals or having ambitions. We can still aspire to do great things. But we learn to build them piece by piece. If an obstacle appears, we do not throw in the towel. We adapt, we reconsider, and we move forward when ready. This approach saves energy and stress. It avoids the burnout that comes from too much haste. It also leads to more thorough results. When we hurry, details get lost. Patience lets us pay attention to the finer points. It leads to careful planning. It fosters steady execution. Over time, we often achieve more this way than with a frantic rush. Paradoxically, by slowing down, we may move further. We let each stage of our work mature before jumping to the next. We reduce the risk of big mistakes that require us to start over. In that sense, patience can speed up progress in the long run.

Some people associate patience with stoicism or numbness. They imagine a patient person as someone who never shows emotion. But true patience does not imply a lack of feeling. We can be patient while still experiencing frustration or sadness. The difference is that we choose not to let those emotions control us. We acknowledge them, and we let them pass in their own time. We wait for clarity before speaking or acting. That wait is the hallmark of patience. It is a conscious decision to pause, even as we feel the rising tide of discomfort. This practice can spare us many regrets. It can help us avoid saying hurtful words in anger. It can keep us from making a rash choice that we later wish to reverse. Instead, we step back, breathe, and examine the situation. Then we respond with a calm mind, or we decide that no immediate response is needed.

On a grander scale, patience can bring stability to world affairs. Large international projects require years of negotiation, planning, and follow-through. If leaders lack patience, deals can collapse. Agreements might be signed hastily, then broken just as quickly. With patience, parties can iron out each detail. They can anticipate challenges and build trust step by step. The resulting partnership stands on stronger ground. Patience also matters in cultural exchange. Understanding another culture takes time. We might need repeated visits, lengthy conversations, and a willingness to see life from unfamiliar angles. Impatient travelers might pass judgment too soon. They might label others as strange without digging deeper. Patient explorers, by contrast, stay curious. They observe and learn before forming conclusions. This fosters genuine connection and respect across borders. It reduces misunderstandings. It leads to more meaningful friendships. In a world that often feels divided, such understanding can be a bridge. That bridge might help prevent conflicts or open doors to new possibilities.

Patience shows up in small personal habits as well. Think about gardening. A seed will not sprout the moment we place it in the soil. It must rest there, absorbing water and nutrients until it is ready. We might see nothing on the surface, yet change is happening below. If we dig it up every day to check, we ruin the process. Patience tells us to trust that growth will happen unseen. Then one day, a tiny green shoot appears. Similarly, cooking often requires patience. Some recipes need slow simmering. If we crank up the heat to finish faster, the food may burn or lose flavor. Writing a book can take many months or years. If the author rushes, the story might remain shallow. These examples remind us that the world operates on many different timelines. We can either fight this reality or learn to flow with it. When we flow, we find peace. We recognize that not everything bends to our clock. We become part of a larger rhythm.

One interesting fact about patience is that it can be strengthened like a muscle. We might think of it as a fixed trait. We see some people who never seem to lose their cool and others who fly off the handle at the slightest wait. However, research suggests that we can develop more patience through mindful practice. Techniques like meditation, mindful breathing, or simply setting small daily goals can help. For instance, we might stand in the longest checkout line on purpose once a week. Then we use that time to observe our thoughts. We notice if we feel restless or annoyed. We remind ourselves that this extra waiting is not going to ruin our day. Over time, this small exercise can lessen our impatience in other situations. We learn that we survive waiting. We even find ways to turn waiting into a chance to reflect or rest. This mindset shift can ripple through every corner of life.

Patience also invites us to respect life's cycles. Each person has their own pace for learning, healing, or maturing. We cannot rush a child through childhood. We cannot force someone to overcome grief by a certain date. We cannot make ourselves master a skill instantly, just because we want to. When we honor these natural rhythms, we become more in tune with reality. We stop fighting the current and start moving with it. This does not mean giving up on guiding ourselves or others. It simply means recognizing that growth has its schedule. That respect keeps us from resenting the process. It also nurtures compassion for those who lag. Instead of mocking them, we remember that everyone is traveling at their speed. In a sense, patience is a humble teacher. It shows us that we are part of a larger order, not the sole master of time.

We can see how patience weaves into other virtues. Patience and kindness go hand in hand. If we are impatient, it is hard to stay kind. We might snap at people or judge them quickly. Patience gives kindness the breathing room to manifest. It also pairs with honesty, because a patient person is often more careful with words. They speak the truth without haste or thoughtless cruelty. It aligns with courage because waiting for something important requires bravery. We might be tempted to give up or settle for less. It takes courage to hold on to a vision. That vision might be a dream job or a just cause. Only patience can sustain us through the trials. Patience also blends with gratitude, because we learn to appreciate small milestones along the way. Instead of feeling upset that we are not yet at the finish line, we notice how far we have come. That gratitude fuels us to keep going. Each step becomes an achievement worth celebrating.

Impatience often arises from a sense of scarcity. We think we do not have enough time. We feel we will miss our chance. But what if we shifted our perspective? What if we saw time as a companion rather than an enemy? Of course, time is finite. We cannot be careless. Yet, rushing does not add more hours to our day. It just floods our nerves with tension. It can even cause accidents or mistakes that cost more time in the end. When we adopt a patient outlook, we become more strategic. We plan with care and then execute our plan steadily. If new information arises, we adjust. We do not panic. We do not blame time itself. Instead, we adapt, staying calm and flexible. This approach can save energy and open up creative solutions we might not see in a hurry. In that sense, patience often leads to efficiency in the long run.

In everyday life, we have many chances to practice patience. We practice it when stuck in a traffic jam. We practice it when teaching a friend to use a computer program. We practice it when waiting for a medical test result. We practice it when saving money for a big purchase. We practice it when learning a new hobby or facing a major decision. Each of these moments offers a small test. Do we succumb to tension and frustration, or do we let patience guide us? Sometimes, we fail the test. We might snap at someone or make a hasty choice. But each mistake becomes a lesson. We see the cost of impatience. We realize how it affects our mood and relationships. Then we can try again. Over time, we become more mindful of our default reactions. We learn to pause and breathe before letting impatience take over.

Patience also allows us to be more present. When we hurry, our mind often races ahead to the next task. We stop noticing what is happening right now. We might miss the beauty of a sunset or the subtle joy of a quiet moment. We might fail to see the shy smile of someone who needs our kindness. Patience slows us down enough to notice. It nudges us to observe details we would otherwise rush past. In doing so, it enriches our experience of life. We might find that we enjoy tasks like washing dishes or folding laundry because we treat them as mindful acts. We let ourselves rest in the moment rather than constantly pushing to finish and move on. This small shift can transform routine chores into pockets of calm. It can make life less frantic and more fulfilling.

In times of adversity, patience provides a source of inner fortitude. We might face a job loss, illness, or heartbreak. Such events can shake our stability. We may want instant recovery or immediate solutions, but that is rarely how life works. Patience helps us accept that healing and rebuilding take time. It encourages us to hold onto faith in the future, even when the present feels grim. It also helps us handle the frustration that comes with setbacks. We learn not to measure progress by one bad day. Instead, we see the bigger picture. We trust that small improvements add up. This mindset protects us from despair. It gives us space to find new perspectives or discover hidden opportunities. Instead of panicking, we calmly explore our options. We lean on supportive people. We keep moving forward step by step.

Another virtue of patience lies in how it fosters deeper understanding. When we are patient with someone's viewpoint, we can learn from them. We can ask questions that uncover more layers. We might find that they have reasons we never considered. If we rushed, we might dismiss them as foolish or uninformed. By waiting and listening, we open the door to empathy. Empathy reduces conflict and reveals common ground. This approach is essential in bridging political or social divides. Quick judgments keep us locked in stereotypes. Patience cracks those walls by allowing for real dialogue. That dialogue might not solve everything, but it can soften hostility. It can lay a foundation for future cooperation. It can remind us that behind every opinion is a person with experiences and feelings. That reminder alone can change how we treat each other.

Ultimately, patience is a gift we give ourselves and others. It protects our peace of mind. It guards our relationships from needless harm. It helps us achieve long-term goals without burning out. It fosters a community based on respect rather than haste. It cultivates resilience in the face of hardship. Yet it is not something we master overnight. It is a practice we return to daily. Sometimes, we might slip back into impatience. We might let anger flare or push for quick results that fail. The key is to forgive ourselves in those moments and try again. Each attempt builds our capacity for patience a bit more. Over a lifetime, that capacity can grow quite large. We may surprise ourselves with how calm we can remain in stressful situations. We might become a source of stability for people around us. We might even inspire them to discover their strength in patience.

Thus, patience stands as a cornerstone of inner peace. It grants us the energy to act wisely. It prevents us from harming ourselves or others through rash decisions. It shows us that life unfolds in many stages, not all of which we can control. It invites us to trust that a seed, once planted, will sprout in its own time. We water it, we care for it, and we wait. That waiting is not a weakness. It is a sign of faith. A sign that we believe in growth, healing, and transformation. No matter how busy or troubled the world becomes, patience remains a timeless ally. It supports us through daily annoyances and major life trials alike. It reminds us that we can find strength in the space between desire and fulfillment. In that space, we learn who we are and what truly matters. We learn that we can be steady, even when the future is uncertain. And in that steadiness, we can discover a kind of power that no rush could ever match.

7. Inner Peace

Inner peace can feel like a gentle glow that warms the heart from the inside. It can guide our thoughts toward calm, even when life brings storms. It often appears in small moments, like watching the sunrise or hearing a soft melody. It does not rely on what we own or how we look. It comes from a deeper place within us, one that is not shaken by passing troubles. People sometimes confuse inner peace with a total absence of problems. But real peace can exist even in the middle of stress. It does not mean ignoring issues. It means understanding that we are more than our worries. It means finding stillness in our core, no matter the chaos outside. When we discover this stillness, we begin to see life more clearly. We respond rather than react. We think before we speak. We feel less hurried. And we sense a quiet strength supporting us.

Inner peace has often been described in spiritual teachings. Many cultures share stories of wise individuals who remain calm when others panic. They do not lose their center, even if events turn harsh. They seem unshakable. Sometimes, we might believe such peace is only for monks or saints. We assume normal people, with bills to pay and schedules to keep, cannot hold onto that depth of calm. Yet, inner peace is not about hiding on a mountaintop. It can live in daily life. It can follow us to work, to school, and even to the grocery store. It simply calls us to pay attention. It asks that we become aware of our mental chatter. Most of us wander through the day with racing minds. We constantly think about what we must do next. We recall past mistakes. We worry about tomorrow. Our minds rarely rest. Inner peace invites us to pause. It whispers that we are allowed to let go of some of those thoughts. By letting go, even for a moment, we create space for calm to enter. That calm can refresh us the way a cool breeze eases a hot day.

This sense of peace influences how we treat others. When we are calm inside, we carry less tension in our words. We become less likely to snap at friends or family. We listen more intently because we are not lost in our noise. We have room to truly hear. This shift can ripple outward. Our calm can help someone else relax. Our steady presence can guide a difficult conversation toward understanding. Over time, these small acts build stronger relationships. Communities where individuals seek inner peace often experience less conflict. People handle differences more gently. They do not rush to insult or blame. They take a breath first. Then they speak with care. This does not erase disagreements. But it lowers the temperature so that people can find ways to move forward together. Inner peace does not mean we never feel anger. It only means we do not let anger own us. We feel it arise, we notice it, we breathe, and we decide how to act. That decision, made in a place of calm, can do wonders. It can prevent hurtful words. It can preserve respect.

There is also a broader social effect when more people find stability within themselves. Imagine an office filled with employees who have at least some measure of inner peace. They remain thoughtful when projects get tough. They do not hurl blame at one another in times of stress. They take responsibility for their tasks. They extend help without expecting praise. This culture can improve the overall quality of the work. It can reduce burnout. It can inspire creativity because people do not feel afraid to share ideas. They know their environment is supportive, not hostile. On a larger scale, entire neighborhoods or cities could benefit if enough residents practiced calm awareness. Politeness in traffic might increase. Discussions on community issues might become more productive. People might volunteer to help neighbors in need, simply because they feel balanced inside. They no longer see the world as a threat. They see it as a shared home. Inner peace can dissolve some of the walls we build out of fear or suspicion.

The importance of inner peace at the personal level is enormous. It affects our health, our mood, and our sense of purpose. Stress is a major factor in many illnesses. When we feel constantly pressured, our bodies release chemicals that, over time, can harm us. We might develop headaches, digestive problems, or trouble sleeping. Inner peace, by reducing chronic stress, can protect our bodies. It can improve immune function. It can help us rest more deeply. It can make us more resilient against everyday irritations. This has been noted in various studies where participants learned relaxation techniques, meditation, or mindfulness. They reported better overall well-being. Their blood pressure often improved. Their anxiety levels dropped. They found they could cope with pain more effectively. Inner peace is not a miracle cure, but it serves as a powerful tool for maintaining both mental and physical health.

Inner peace also guides us to make wiser decisions. When we act from a place of turmoil, we often choose what offers quick relief. We might snap at people, avoid responsibilities, or chase shallow pleasures just to escape our tensions. But when we feel calm, we see the bigger picture. We weigh the pros and cons with patience. We consider the impact of our actions on ourselves and others. We think about the future as well as the present. We do not seek the easy way out, but the path that aligns with our values. That path might require effort, but it satisfies us at a deeper level. This approach can transform our careers, our relationships, and our personal growth. We stop running in circles. We move forward with clarity.

Challenges can block us from finding inner peace. One major obstacle is the pace of modern life. We are bombarded with tasks, notifications, and endless stimuli. We might feel we have no time to pause. Our days might look like one giant to-do list. We might measure success by how busy we are. Another challenge is the fear of facing ourselves. True inner peace demands some self-reflection. We need to look at our insecurities, regrets, or hidden wounds. That can be uncomfortable. Many would rather stay distracted. They do not want to face those inner shadows. Yet, to find real calm, we must acknowledge the parts of us that ache or feel ashamed. We must befriend them rather than deny them. This step can be hard, but it is key to healing. Another challenge is external pressure. Society may tell us that being calm and reflective is weak. It might push us to compete or to accumulate more stuff. We might wonder if seeking peace is selfish, especially when the world has so many problems. But genuine peace in one heart can eventually benefit others. A stable mind is more capable of effective action. It is also less likely to contribute to the chaos.

A lesser-known fact about inner peace is how it can boost creativity. Studies suggest that people who practice calming methods often reach creative solutions faster. Their minds are not cluttered with anxiety. They can think more flexibly. They can see connections that stress might obscure. Another interesting point is how peace can influence our relationships with animals. We often see that pets or other creatures sense our mood. If we are anxious, they might react with unease. If we are calm, they might be calmer around us. Some animal trainers rely heavily on their sense of peace to communicate non-verbally. This demonstrates that inner calm can extend beyond human interactions. It can shape how we interact with all forms of life. Another curious insight is how inner peace can slow our perception of time. When we are stressed, time rushes by in a blur. We feel we never have enough. In moments of calm, time seems more expansive. We notice details and live more fully in each second. This can make life richer and more memorable. It is as though peace opens a hidden door to the present moment, one we often overlook when in a rush.

Inner peace is important also because it lays a foundation for empathy. When our minds are in constant turmoil, we have little bandwidth to care about others. We are too busy dealing with our stress. But a calm mind has room to notice someone else's pain. We can pause, listen, and help. This empathy can spark acts of kindness that create a chain reaction. One small gesture can lead to another, eventually improving many lives. Inner peace also plays a role in personal resilience. We will face losses in life. We might lose a job, a friendship, or a loved one. These events can shatter us if we are not grounded. Inner peace helps us remain upright. It does not remove grief or sadness, but it supports us as we mourn. It keeps us from drowning in despair. We trust that our core is steady, even if our hearts ache. We allow ourselves to feel sorrow without believing it is the only truth. Gradually, this approach helps us heal. We recover and re-engage with life, carrying the lessons we learned.

There are many paths to inner peace. Some find it through prayer or meditation. Others discover it in nature. They walk among trees, feel the wind, and realize they are part of something vast. Some find calm in creative hobbies, like painting or playing music. Others find it in yoga or martial arts, where the mind and body move in harmony. Still, others cultivate peace by helping others, losing themselves in service. Each path can lead to the same center: a place where our thoughts and emotions rest without constant struggle. The key is consistency. A single walk in the woods might bring fleeting calm. But lasting inner peace often requires regular practice, whether that is daily meditation or a weekly outdoor visit. Over time, these practices reshape our mental patterns. We form habits of awareness. We learn to recognize when stress begins to build. We develop ways to release it before it overwhelms us. This slow, steady process can yield strong results.

The social impact of inner peace grows as more people adopt these practices. Imagine if schools taught basic methods for calming the mind. Children would learn to focus their attention, handle conflicts with reflection, and manage their emotions more healthily. Bullying might decrease, while academic performance could rise because students can concentrate better. Teachers might find their classrooms more cooperative. In workplaces, simple group sessions for relaxation or mindfulness can reduce turnover. They can cut down on sick days caused by stress. They can create a positive culture that benefits both staff and leadership. Society as a whole might notice less aggression in public spaces. People would stand in line with more patience. They would drive with less road rage. They might approach differences of opinion without turning to insults. Over time, these shifts could transform the emotional climate of an entire region. It might seem idealistic, but small efforts at inner peace do add up.

At the personal level, the importance of finding this calm cannot be overstated. It shapes our sense of who we are. It reveals that we do not have to be ruled by every wave of emotion. We can choose a centered response. This sense of choice boosts self-esteem. It affirms that we have agency in our mental landscape. It also helps us break unhealthy cycles. Perhaps we grew up in a household of constant conflict. We might feel doomed to repeat those patterns. Inner peace training can interrupt that cycle. It shows us there is a different way. We learn to pause, breathe, and handle tensions calmly. This new approach can then be passed on to our children or friends, opening the door to better relationships.

One challenge many face is thinking that inner peace means ignoring reality. They worry they will become passive if they focus on calm. But true peace involves clarity, not denial. We can see problems for what they are while refusing to drown in panic or anger. A calm mind can be more effective in problem-solving. It can gather facts, evaluate them, and act with precision. It avoids the extremes of panic or rage, which often lead to impulsive mistakes. Peaceful does not mean inactive. It means centered, thoughtful, and balanced. Another hurdle is the misconception that we need a perfect environment for peace. People say, "I'll be calm when I get a better job or when I retire." But outer conditions do not guarantee inner stability. Yes, certain changes can help us feel less stressed. Yet, if we do not train the mind, even the most peaceful place can become stressful once we bring our anxieties there. Inner peace is an inner skill. It can thrive in busy cities or quiet countryside settings. It depends on our outlook rather than external details.

Sometimes, our past trauma can block our path to calm. We might carry deep emotional scars that make sitting quietly feel unsafe. In such cases, professional help can be invaluable. Therapists or counselors trained in trauma-informed practices can guide us to process those wounds gently. They can suggest techniques that nurture both safety and calm. Over time, even deep scars can heal enough for peace to emerge. This journey might be slow, and that is okay. Each small step matters. The end goal is not to erase the past but to relate to it without being controlled by it. Inner peace becomes the ground on which we can walk forward, free from the old chains.

A lesser-known aspect of finding inner peace is the idea of non-attachment. This does not mean we stop caring. It means we stop clinging. We stop demanding that life must always follow our script. We learn to accept change. We see that people come and go. We realize that trying to control everything only creates tension. This non-attachment helps us flow with the rhythms of life. We do our best without insisting on a particular outcome. This does not kill ambition. It refines it. We work toward goals with passion but remain flexible if plans shift. This flexibility spares us needless suffering. It helps us adapt when reality differs from our hopes. We still feel disappointment or sadness at times, but we do not become paralyzed by them. We remain anchored to the peace within, trusting that we can handle the next wave when it arrives.

Another side of inner peace is how it grants us a sense of wholeness. Many people walk through life feeling that something is missing. They chase experiences or possessions to fill a void. Yet, those external additions rarely satisfy for long. Real contentment grows from an inner well. When we learn to connect with that quiet center, we realize we are enough. We do not need endless distractions to prove our worth. We do not need constant reassurance from others. That does not mean we become anti-social. We still value relationships, but we do not depend on them for our core sense of self. This independence can strengthen friendships and romances because we are with others by choice, not desperation. We share our peace with them instead of demanding they fix our emptiness.

Inner peace also reveals the power of living in the present moment. We spend so much time regretting the past or worrying about the future. In doing so, we miss the only time we ever truly have: right now. When we practice returning our awareness to the present, we break the cycle of regret and anxiety. We notice small beauties, like the taste of our morning coffee or the sound of rain on the window. This appreciation for simple details can lift our mood. It can also make us more effective in what we do. Whether we are writing an email or washing dishes, being fully present improves our skills and reduces errors. Our minds stop drifting. We feel alive and connected to the task at hand. Over time, these mini-moments of presence accumulate into a more peaceful day, and then a more peaceful life.

Inner peace can also transform how we deal with fear. Fear thrives on the unknown. We imagine worst-case scenarios and scare ourselves. But a calm mind can look at fear with curiosity. It asks, "Is this fear real right now, or is it just a thought?" It seems that many worries never come to pass. By staying grounded, we can analyze risk more accurately. We can prepare for valid dangers without being overwhelmed by imaginary ones. This balanced approach to fear keeps us from panic while ensuring we stay safe. It also leaves room for courage. We can take measured risks in pursuit of dreams, knowing we can handle setbacks if they occur. That sense of readiness arises from the knowledge that inner peace will support us, whatever happens.

The ripple effects of inner peace are far-reaching. They can enhance community well-being, improve family bonds, and boost personal growth. They can also gently shift global consciousness, one person at a time. Each peaceful mind is like a calm lake in a storm. It reflects clarity. It offers refuge to those around it. If enough lakes remain still, the landscape of the entire region changes. Conflict might not vanish, but it loses some force. People remember that there is another way to live. This possibility can encourage them to explore their inner path. That is how peace can spread silently, beyond social media debates or political platforms. It grows from within each individual, shining outward through countless small gestures of kindness and understanding.

Maintaining inner peace is a continual process. Some days, we might feel centered and relaxed. Other days, we wake up tense or face unexpected hardships that rattle us. This is normal. Peace is not a final destination, but a practice we keep refining. When we notice we are off-balance, we return to our methods. Maybe we sit for a brief meditation, or we take a slow walk in the fresh air. Maybe we talk with a trusted friend, or we write in a journal. Gradually, we find our center again. This cycle repeats. Over time, the periods of peace can grow longer, and the times of turmoil can feel less crushing. We learn to recover more quickly. We accept that we are human and prone to ups and downs. This acceptance itself brings gentleness. It keeps us from demanding constant perfection.

Inner peace often aligns with a greater sense of compassion for the world. As we calm our storms, we develop a desire to help calm the storms of others. We see that many conflicts arise from fear or pain. We see how often people act out because they cannot find their peace. This realization can spark empathy rather than judgment. We might become inspired to volunteer, donate, or engage in community projects. We might share our peaceful presence with those who are lonely or distressed. We might speak kindly to someone who feels misunderstood. These acts extend the warmth of our inner calm to those around us. This extension can plant seeds of hope and healing, even if we do not see immediate results. The important thing is that our peace does not remain locked within us. It flows outward, touching others in subtle yet significant ways.

In the end, inner peace is more than just a pleasant feeling. It is a way of life that impacts every corner of our reality. It shapes our interactions at home, at work, and in the broader community. It influences our physical health, our emotional resilience, and our sense of purpose. It can open the door to creativity and to deeper compassion. It can soften the edges of fear and anger. It can remind us that we are enough, just as we are. This reminder can free us from chasing endless goals that are never satisfying. It brings us back to the present, where we can truly live. And in that presence, we may find that all the riches we ever sought have been within us all along. Inner peace is not about escaping life's duties or ignoring pain. It is about facing them with a steady heart, confident in our ability to remain whole. It is about trusting that beneath our shifting moods and thoughts lies a reservoir of calm. If we can learn to tap that reservoir, we can move through the world with grace. We can be a source of comfort and wisdom for ourselves and for those around us. We can stand firm when hardships arise, and we can celebrate joy without clinging. This gift of peace is available to every human being, regardless of background or belief. It asks only that we turn our attention inward and treat ourselves with kindness. Once we do, we may find that life grows richer, and we, in turn, become beacons of calm in a restless world.

8. Respect's Power

Respect can shape our lives in ways we often overlook. It is not just about being polite. It is an attitude that values the worth of every individual. It goes beyond simple manners or rigid rules. It begins deep inside the heart. When we respect someone, we acknowledge their dignity. We show we see them as human, equal in value to ourselves. That sense of equality breaks barriers. It can heal emotional wounds before they fester into bitterness. It can open lines of communication that once seemed locked. It can prevent small disagreements from becoming deep rifts. In a world that sometimes seems dominated by self-interest, respect can be a bright thread linking us all. This is not a minor detail of social etiquette. It is a powerful force that can reshape relationships, communities, and entire cultures.

Respect shows up in many forms. Sometimes, it is a simple act of listening without interruption. It can be the choice to speak in a considerate tone, even when emotions are high. It can be the decision to honor someone's personal space or their property. It also includes respecting ourselves and recognizing our value. Many of us grew up hearing phrases like "treat others as you want to be treated." That statement sums up the core of respect. It suggests empathy, putting ourselves in the shoes of the person before us. This empathy helps us grasp the impact our words or actions might have. From that awareness, respect naturally flows.

Socially, respect can have dramatic impacts. In schools, respectful behavior among students can reduce bullying. It can build a safer environment where kids feel free to learn and explore. In workplaces, respect can ease tension and promote teamwork. People who feel respected at work are more inclined to share ideas openly. They trust their colleagues and superiors. That trust can lead to creative problem-solving. It can reduce conflicts. It can make an organization function more smoothly. On a broader level, respect can help people from different cultures or backgrounds find common ground. They might not agree on everything. Yet, if they see each other's humanity, they can talk without turning disagreements into hatred. Over time, this outlook can prevent deep divisions from tearing communities apart.

Respect also plays a key role in family life. When family members respect each other, even routine tasks can become opportunities for bonding. They approach disagreements by aiming to solve them, not to humiliate or dominate. Parents who show respect to their children teach them a powerful lesson. Those children learn to see themselves as worthy. They also learn to extend that courtesy to others. They may grow up better equipped to form healthy friendships. They learn how to communicate without resorting to insults. That early foundation can shape their entire adult life. It can set a pattern of positive relationships. It can reduce the chance of toxic dynamics repeating across generations.

There is also an inward dimension to respect. Many people think of respect as something we show to others. But it often begins with self-respect. That means recognizing our value. It means treating ourselves with kindness. It is not about being self-centered or arrogant. It is about acknowledging that we, like all other human beings, have worth. When we believe this, we become less likely to let others disrespect us. We draw healthy boundaries. We do not accept abuse or neglect. We also become more aware of how we treat our bodies and minds. If we respect ourselves, we might choose healthier habits. We might avoid self-destructive behaviors. We might push ourselves to grow, but not in a punishing way. This self-respect then radiates outward. It shows in the way we hold ourselves, speak, and even smile.

Respect carries importance because it is tied to basic human dignity. Every individual, no matter their station in life, deserves a baseline of respectful treatment. It does not mean we must agree with them or support their choices. It means we acknowledge they are human beings with feelings, needs, and experiences. By embracing this stance, we open doors to compassion. We remind ourselves that we share the world with countless others who are, in some essential way, like us. They want peace, comfort, and understanding. When we keep that truth in mind, it is harder to harm or belittle them. Over time, the idea of respect can shape our moral compass, influencing decisions we make at home, at work, or in society.

When we think about respect, we often picture polite words. Yet, it goes deeper than language. It includes body language, eye contact, and tone of voice. Sometimes, we might say something polite, but our posture or facial expression reveals contempt. That is not true respect. True respect is sincere. It arises from genuine regard for someone's value. It does not require us to like them or share their views. We can still respect someone even if we find their opinions troubling. We can do so by separating the person from the ideas they hold. We can choose to address the ideas in a firm, constructive way without attacking their dignity. This approach can create possibilities for dialogue, even in tense situations. It can keep us from sinking into name-calling or cruelty.

Many challenges block the path of respect. One is anger. When we feel angry, we can be quick to lash out. We might forget that the other person also feels pain or confusion. We focus on our frustration. We say or do hurtful things, which can spark a cycle of conflict. Another challenge is fear. Sometimes, we fear those who are different from us. We do not understand their culture or their beliefs, so we belittle them or treat them as lesser. This behavior often arises from ignorance or deeply ingrained biases. It can lead to prejudice, discrimination, or even violence. Another challenge is ego. We might place our own needs or pride so high that we fail to see the worth of those around us. We might think we deserve special treatment at the expense of others. This can show up in daily life, like cutting in line or dismissing a colleague's viewpoint. In the long run, that attitude creates tension and resentment.

An interesting aspect of respect is how it ties to listening. True respect involves not just hearing words, but giving them real attention. Many people listen only to plan their reply. They do not absorb what the other person says. Respectful listening puts our agenda on pause. We focus on understanding. This might sound simple, but it requires practice. It can be hard to set aside our immediate reactions. Yet, when we manage to do it, the other person feels seen. They sense that we care about their perspective. This can defuse anger or suspicion. It can lead to insights we might have missed otherwise. It can build trust, which is essential for any healthy relationship, whether personal or professional.

There are also little-known facts about respect. One of them is how it can influence psychological well-being. People who feel respected by those around them tend to have higher self-esteem. They perform better in group tasks. They recover faster from setbacks because they know they have a safety net of support. Another interesting point is that respect can reduce stress. Tensions rise when we fear being judged or humiliated. But in a respectful environment, people feel safer to express concerns, ask for help, or admit mistakes. This safety can improve learning and productivity. It can also foster creativity, as individuals are less afraid to propose new ideas. Respect even ties into conflict resolution. Many mediators have found that once both sides show respect for each other, progress becomes possible. The barriers of hostility start to fall. People open their minds to compromise because they no longer feel they must defend their basic worth.

Respect holds a crucial place in leadership. A leader who respects the team earns loyalty more naturally. People follow them because they feel valued, not just out of fear or obligation. Such a leader listens to input, shares credit for success, and communicates transparently. These behaviors show respect for people's intelligence and efforts. In contrast, a leader who shows disrespect might bully, belittle, or dictate every detail. That approach can spark resentment. People might comply in the short term but will not go the extra mile. Over time, the team's morale drops. Turnover rates may rise. Productivity suffers. In many studies, employees rank feeling respected at work as highly as receiving competitive pay. That reveals how deeply people need to sense that they matter.

Respect can also be seen in global relations. Nations that respect each other's sovereignty and culture are more likely to form lasting alliances. They may still have disagreements over trade or policy. Yet, they work through these with negotiation and diplomacy. Conversely, if a nation treats another with contempt or tries to impose its will, conflicts can escalate quickly. On an individual level, travelers who visit new places often discover the power of respect. A humble attitude, a willingness to learn local customs, and a courteous approach can open doors. Locals may respond with kindness and guidance. That mutual respect can lead to friendships that cross language barriers. It can also help reduce stereotypes. Even in areas where tension runs high, respectful behavior can shield visitors from hostility.

Within communities, respect can bridge generation gaps. Younger people may feel misunderstood by older generations, and vice versa. When each side decides to treat the other with dignity, real communication can begin. The young can learn from the elder's experience. The elder can learn from the young's fresh outlook. This two-way exchange keeps societies balanced. It also preserves valuable traditions while welcoming new ideas. Without respect, these interactions might dissolve into eye-rolling or stubborn lectures. Both sides lose the chance to grow and learn from each other.

There is also a link between respect and environmental stewardship. When we extend respect beyond human relationships, we see nature as worthy of care. We realize the land, water, and air sustain our lives. If we treat the planet with disregard, we harm ourselves in the end. Respect for nature might show in small acts, like recycling or reducing waste. It might appear in bigger choices, like supporting policies that protect forests or oceans. This broader understanding of respect enlarges our moral scope. We see that everything is connected. Our well-being depends on the well-being of the ecosystems around us. This viewpoint can inspire more responsible behavior at both individual and collective levels.

Respect can also shape personal ethics. When we commit to respecting others, we might reassess our opinions. We might notice we have unconscious biases toward certain groups. That realization can be uncomfortable. But by confronting it, we grow. We challenge ourselves to do better. We question stereotypes we picked up from media or family myths. We learn about people's experiences directly, rather than relying on rumors. Over time, that process can transform our worldview. We become more open-minded and less quick to judge. We see the humanity in those who once seemed alien or even threatening.

This shift often brings social rewards. People sense when we are genuinely respectful. They relax around us. They may be more willing to share their stories or invite us into their circles. Respect fosters connections that last. It can even help us resolve old grudges. Perhaps there was someone we resented for a long time. By showing them a measure of respect, we might open a door to dialogue. Maybe we discover we misunderstood their motives. Or we find a shared interest that forms a bridge. Respect does not mean we must become best friends with everyone. However, it does allow for peaceful coexistence, which can reduce stress and tension.

That peaceful coexistence contributes to a larger sense of well-being. In communities that prioritize respect, daily life feels less chaotic. People are more likely to greet each other warmly, show courtesy in shared spaces, and act with civility during disagreements. This environment supports mental health. It can help reduce aggression, vandalism, or random acts of violence. Without respect, frustration can boil over into destructive behavior. That negativity then spreads, causing more damage. But with respect, there is a sense of stability. People know that their basic dignity is safe. That safety is precious. It allows them to flourish, contribute their talents, and help others do the same.

Some people worry that showing respect means giving up their power. They think that if they treat someone as an equal, they lose authority or control. But real respect can enhance legitimate authority. When a person in charge respects their team, the team respects them back. This mutual bond is much stronger than one built on fear. A respectful leader can direct a group with fewer rebellions. Their instructions carry weight because the members trust their intentions. Even among peers, respect does not mean weakening oneself. It means choosing to see the good in others. This choice often leads to better cooperation, making everyone stronger. It does not require us to surrender our goals or boundaries. We can respectfully say no when needed. We can maintain our principles while still treating others courteously.

There is also a spiritual or moral dimension to respect. Many belief systems teach that all life is sacred. They encourage followers to approach others with reverence. This can include offering a hand to a stranger or refraining from hateful words. These teachings are not restricted to one religion. They appear in different forms across cultures. They often highlight the unity of humanity. Respect becomes a way to honor the divine spark in each person or the shared breath of life. Even for those without formal religious practice, the idea that each person deserves humane treatment can feel profound. It resonates on a basic human level.

Respect sometimes requires courage. We might have to stand up for someone who is being ridiculed, even if we risk mockery ourselves. We might have to speak out against unfair policies at work, despite the risk of backlash. We might have to confront our circle if they belittle someone behind their back. These moments test our commitment to respect. They show if it is a principle we hold dear or just a polite façade. Real respect is not always easy. It may challenge social norms. It may place us in uncomfortable positions. But by holding fast, we strengthen our character. We become more aligned with our deepest values. That alignment creates inner harmony, which can foster a sense of peace and confidence in our actions.

There are many simple ways to practice respect daily. We can let others finish talking before we respond. We can use polite language and watch our tone, even under stress. We can acknowledge people's achievements rather than take them for granted. We can ask for opinions and truly consider them. We can handle property with care, even if it is not ours. We can also respect boundaries, whether physical or emotional. That means not pressuring someone to share more than they want or to do something against their will. In a digital sense, it might mean not sharing private information without permission. Each of these small acts can reinforce a culture of respect around us.

That culture of respect can extend to disagreement. We can learn to debate ideas without insulting the people who hold them. We can focus on evidence rather than personal attacks. We can be firm in our stance while preserving the other person's dignity. This can feel tricky, especially in heated topics. Yet it is possible. By doing this, we keep dialogue open. We create room for mutual discovery. Even if we never see eye to eye, we can still maintain a level of civility that preserves peace. This might seem like a lost art, but it is within reach if we value respect enough to practice it.

When we lack respect, the consequences can be severe. Relationships can break down. Families can splinter. Communities can become hostile. Workplaces can turn toxic. People lose trust in each other. They become more defensive. They may lash out or isolate themselves. Over time, this can lead to larger social rifts. Hate speech or prejudice can thrive where respect is absent. That hate can erupt into abuse or violence. By contrast, a foundation of mutual respect can de-escalate tension. It can help people address conflicts before they spiral out of control. It does not solve every problem, but it sets a tone for healthier communication and problem-solving.

Respect also plays a big role in personal self-worth. When we see others treating us with courtesy and acknowledging our viewpoints, we feel validated. We are more likely to believe that we matter. This belief can fuel growth and personal development. We dare to try new things because we trust that failing will not make us worthless. We learn from mistakes and move on. Lack of respect can have the opposite effect. We might doubt our abilities. We might withdraw from opportunities. We might struggle with shame or self-doubt. Overcoming that damage can take a long time. It might require counseling or supportive friends who rebuild our sense of worth. All of this shows that respect is not just a social nicety. It has a direct impact on emotional health.

In a broader sense, respect is part of the journey to inner peace. When we respect ourselves, we create calm within. We stop the cycle of harsh self-judgment. We treat our mind and body with gentleness. This inner gentleness extends outward, making us kinder to others. That external kindness, in turn, enhances our relationships. We face fewer conflicts. We experience less guilt from hurting others' feelings. We gain a sense that the world is safer and more cooperative. This sense can reduce anxiety and stress. We begin to believe that even in disagreements, a respectful dialogue is possible. That belief helps us maintain our center in difficult times. It also encourages us to be proactive in building respectful communities.

If we imagine a society where respect is the norm, we might see people greeting each other warmly. We might see open forums where diverse opinions are shared without insult. We might see leaders who listen carefully to the concerns of citizens. We might see families that gather around a table and discuss issues patiently. We might see the environment treated as a shared responsibility. We might see differences in religion, race, or politics handled with humility rather than contempt. This might sound idealistic. Yet each of us can move in that direction. Each small act of respect is a step on that path.

Sometimes, people wonder if respect can be faked. They might say polite words but harbor hate inside. Such an approach might temporarily prevent conflict, but it will not build true harmony. Fake respect can collapse if tension rises. Authentic respect grows from a genuine understanding that others have value. This understanding can evolve. We might start by simply acting politely, then over time realize the depth of our shared humanity. That realization can shift our feelings. Our politeness becomes a natural expression of care. In that shift, we find the real power of respect. It fosters not just polite behavior, but actual mutual regard. That mutual regard can create bonds that outlast superficial differences.

Respect is powerful because it is universal. It cuts across language barriers. A gentle nod, a welcoming smile, or a considerate gesture can speak volumes without words. People recognize respect in how we handle a conversation, in how we respond to frustration, in whether we keep our promises or treat property carefully. They sense whether we see them as equal human beings. That sense often determines how they respond to us. If they detect disrespect, they might close off or become hostile. If they sense respect, they become more open. This is why respect is often described as a key to effective communication. It unlocks cooperation and understanding where it might not have existed before.

In daily life, respect can appear in subtle ways. Holding a door open for someone, letting another driver merge, or offering a seat to an elderly person are small gestures, but they matter. They say, "I notice you. I value your comfort." This fosters a positive atmosphere in public spaces. Similarly, respecting someone's time is another way. Showing up punctually, or if we are late, informing them with an apology acknowledges their schedule. It says we do not view their time as trivial. Respect can also mean asking for consent before sharing details about another person's life. It can mean giving them credit for an idea. Each of these acts might feel minor. Yet, when many people do them, the collective result is significant. It forms a culture of respect.

When conflicts arise, respect guides us to solve them responsibly. We avoid personal attacks. We avoid generalizing negative traits. We avoid mocking or humiliating the other side. Instead, we focus on the core issue. We try to see the reasoning behind their stance. We present our points without arrogance. This approach can save both sides a great deal of pain. It makes it more likely that they will remain open to each other's input. It does not guarantee full agreement, but it prevents the situation from devolving into hostility. Even if we must walk away without a solution, we do so without destroying trust. This leaves room for future dialogue, which might eventually lead to a breakthrough.

Ultimately, respect uplifts our sense of shared humanity. It reminds us that, beneath differences in culture or opinion, we all share the need to be treated with dignity. This realization can cut through many forms of division. It can help us see that empathy, patience, and kindness are not signs of weakness, but signs of maturity. They demonstrate that we grasp the profound truth that each person has inherent worth. When we live by that truth, we align ourselves with a force that can transform hearts. It can replace hostility with cooperation. It can turn suspicion into curiosity. It can bring families and communities closer together. And it can pave the way for a peaceful, more harmonious future.

In this sense, respect is not just a social rule. It is a powerful path. It can lead us toward greater understanding, compassion, and unity. It can help us stand firm in our own identity while granting others the freedom to be who they are. It prevents us from viewing the world through a narrow lens of "us versus them." Instead, it shows us the larger family of humanity. That understanding can help us find solutions to shared problems. It can remind us that cooperation is more fruitful than conflict. And as we walk this path, we discover that respect enriches our own inner life. We feel calmer, more balanced, and more connected to the people around us. We see that each person, in their way, contributes to the tapestry of existence. We can appreciate them for it. That appreciation fills us with humility and gratitude, key ingredients of a peaceful heart.

9. Transforming Anger

Anger can feel like a sharp flame that bursts inside the mind. It can rise in an instant when we feel hurt, threatened, or ignored. Often, it emerges when we sense something unfair or insulting. This emotion has many faces. Sometimes it flickers quietly, and we only notice its heat. Other times, it roars like wildfire, overwhelming our thoughts. Anger by itself is not good or bad. It is a signal that something feels wrong. But if we do not handle it wisely, it can push us to act in ways we later regret. It can lead to harsh words or destructive behaviors. It can damage relationships that matter to us. That is why transforming anger is so important. We can learn to use its energy in a way that helps rather than harms.

Many people see anger as a force that must be suppressed. They try to shove it down and pretend it does not exist. Others let it explode in unfiltered rage. They break things or say words they cannot take back. Both extremes can cause harm. Suppressing anger can turn it into a hidden poison. We might start to feel constant tension in our bodies. We might develop stress-related problems. We might also let bitterness grow until it erupts in destructive ways. On the other hand, letting anger reign free can destroy trust with those we love. It can also leave us feeling shame afterward. Neither path truly resolves the source of the anger. Neither path helps us grow. True transformation of anger is different. It requires noticing the feeling and stepping back to understand its roots. It asks us to find healthier ways to channel that powerful energy.

Anger can serve a purpose. It alerts us to threats or injustices. It can motivate us to defend ourselves or someone else who is vulnerable. It can give us the courage to confront a problem head-on. In this sense, anger can be a catalyst for positive change. Many social movements have roots in righteous anger against oppression. Yet, the real challenge is learning to express anger without letting it consume us. When we master that, anger can become a tool for good. It can fuel determination instead of lashing out blindly. It can focus our minds on the steps needed to address the root cause. That is when we see anger transform from a destructive fire into a guiding flame. But this shift takes effort. It also takes practice.

There are many reasons anger emerges. We might feel attacked, humiliated, or powerless. We might resent being overlooked or disrespected. Sometimes, anger masks deeper emotions like sadness or fear. For instance, if someone breaks our trust, the heartbreak might be too painful to face. So we turn it into anger instead because anger feels stronger than sadness. Recognizing these hidden layers helps us understand ourselves better. We might discover we are carrying old wounds. We might learn we have beliefs about how we should be treated. When those beliefs are challenged, anger flares. If we never look deeper, we stay stuck in a cycle. We keep getting angry for similar reasons without knowing why. That can strain our relationships and lower our quality of life.

Anger has a social impact. In families, it can shape how children learn to handle conflict. If parents explode in fury or give each other the silent treatment, children pick up those patterns. They might grow up believing that is how everyone reacts when upset. These habits can then pass through generations. That is why learning to transform anger can change entire family dynamics. It can break cycles of aggressive communication. In workplaces, anger can create toxic atmospheres. It can lead to fear, tension, or passive-aggressive behaviors. Productivity can fall because people dread interactions. On a wider scale, collective anger can stir unrest in communities. It can lead to riots if it remains unchecked. Yet, if people channel that anger into dialogue and constructive action, it can bring about reforms. It can highlight systemic problems. This is why it is crucial to understand anger rather than simply judging it as bad.

The importance of transforming anger is also tied to mental and physical health. Chronic anger can increase blood pressure. It can flood the body with stress hormones like cortisol. Over time, this wears down our systems. We might experience headaches, disrupted sleep, or digestive issues. Emotionally, unprocessed anger can lead to constant irritability. We might snap at minor inconveniences. We might isolate ourselves because we feel misunderstood. If the anger becomes too heavy, it can even turn inward into depression. On the flip side, learning to process anger in a balanced way can reduce stress. It can improve relationships and open space for healthier coping. It can make us more patient and empathetic. This shift can bring more harmony into daily life.

The challenges to transforming anger are many. One is the instinctive reaction we have at the moment. When anger hits, our heart rate speeds up. Our muscles tense. We feel that urge to fight or flee. Pausing to reflect can feel unnatural. Another challenge is the fear of vulnerability. Some of us feel that if we do not appear strong and angry, others will take advantage. Another obstacle is a lack of role models. We might not have seen people who handle anger calmly and assertively. Instead, we might have grown up around people who either explode or bury their anger. In addition, the constant pressures of life add fuel to the fire. Stress at work, financial worries, or unresolved trauma can make anger flare more easily. These challenges do not mean transformation is impossible. They simply highlight why it can be hard. A deliberate effort is needed.

A lesser-known fact about anger is that it often passes quickly if we do not feed it. Research suggests that strong anger can dissolve within about 90 seconds when we stop ruminating on it. That means if we notice the wave of anger and let it rise and fall, it might fade on its own. But what usually happens is we keep thinking about what made us angry. We rehearse the injustice in our minds. We imagine all the cutting remarks we could make. This mental repetition keeps anger alive. Another intriguing point is how anger can sometimes hide feelings of helplessness or anxiety. People who struggle with fear might find anger more tolerable. Acting angry makes them feel more in control. Yet, behind the rage is a sense of vulnerability. Recognizing this pattern can lead to deeper healing.

It helps to have concrete strategies for working with anger. One approach is to name the emotion in the moment. We mentally say, "I feel anger rising now." This small act of labeling can prevent us from becoming lost in the feeling. Next, we can pause and breathe. Slow, deep breaths send a signal to the body to calm down. This does not make the anger vanish, but it gives us a bit of space. Another method is to step away briefly if the situation allows it. Going for a short walk or sipping water can give us time to think before speaking. We can ask ourselves what is causing the anger. Is it a sense of disrespect? Is it fear of losing control? This self-inquiry can reveal the deeper layers. Once we see the cause, we can address it more constructively.

Transforming anger also involves expressing it appropriately. This might mean talking to the person who upset us but doing so with clear, respectful words. We describe the action that hurt us and how it made us feel. We avoid personal attacks like name-calling. Instead, we focus on the issue. This practice helps us stand up for ourselves without destroying relationships. In some cases, writing in a journal can help. We can pour out our anger on paper, which is safe. We do not harm anyone with our words. Afterward, we might find we have a clearer sense of what to do next. Another tool is physical activity. Exercise can help burn off the adrenaline rush that comes with anger. A walk, a run, or even a round of jumping jacks can shift our energy. The key is to do it mindfully, aware that we are releasing tension.

There is also a social aspect to transforming anger. We can create environments where open communication is valued. In families, for example, establishing a habit of regular check-ins can help. Each member can share something that's bothering them in a calm setting.

This prevents issues from building up until anger explodes. In workplaces, leaders can model healthy conflict resolution. They can encourage employees to express disagreements in respectful ways. They can also provide training in communication skills. These steps can reduce the chances of anger turning into feuds that hurt morale. In communities, workshops or support groups can teach anger management. They can show people that it is not a sign of weakness to seek help for emotional struggles. These measures can lead to fewer violent incidents. They can also foster a culture of empathy.

The importance of transforming anger also appears in how we approach activism and social causes. Many people feel angry about injustices in society. This anger can spur them to protest or organize. The challenge is to keep the movement constructive. If anger remains the sole driving force, it can become destructive. Riots or harmful rhetoric can overshadow the original message. But if that anger is channeled into structured campaigns, it can lead to meaningful reforms. Leaders who know how to harness anger for good can focus public attention on problems. They can push for laws or policies that address root causes. This is how a personal emotion can evolve into a collective transformation. But it demands emotional discipline and a willingness to work with others respectfully.

Some believe that anger is never useful. They see it as a negative emotion that should be eradicated. Others argue that anger can serve a vital role in alerting us to harm. Perhaps the truth lies somewhere in between. Anger itself is neither purely good nor purely bad. It depends on how it is handled. Left unchecked, it can be toxic. Guided with care, it can help us stand for our rights and others' rights. It can help us correct wrongs. It can also teach us about boundaries, reminding us that certain lines should not be crossed. Over time, we learn to distinguish righteous anger from mere impatience or wounded pride. That distinction helps us direct our energy more wisely.

We might wonder what it means to transform anger spiritually. Some traditions encourage compassion for the one who caused the anger. They suggest we try to see that person's humanity. Perhaps they acted out of ignorance or their pain. This perspective does not mean accepting harmful behavior. But it can reduce the hatred that often accompanies anger. It can keep us from seeking revenge. It can guide us toward seeking solutions that help everyone learn. Another angle is to reflect on impermanence. We realize the situation that sparked our anger may not last. Even if it feels huge now, life moves on. This reflection can shrink the anger's hold on us.

Anger and forgiveness also share a complex relationship. Some see forgiveness as dismissing the wrong done. That is not necessarily the case. Forgiveness can be a choice we make to free ourselves from the chains of resentment. It does not excuse the harmful act. It also does not mean we must remain close to the person who hurt us. Instead, it means letting go of the burning desire to punish. It means deciding not to carry that anger forever. This process can be challenging. At times, our anger feels justified. But holding onto it for a long time can drain our energy. It can poison our mood. By choosing to transform that anger into understanding, we create room for healing. This healing might happen slowly, step by step. But each step can bring relief.

Anger can also be transformed through art. Painting, writing poetry, or playing music can channel strong emotions into creativity. Many powerful works of art emerged from intense anger about injustice, heartbreak, or oppression. The act of creation can soothe the inner flames. It can bring meaning to pain. It can communicate a message without violence. In the same way, comedic expressions can help. Sometimes, turning a frustrating experience into humor can defuse it. We see the absurd side and find ourselves laughing. That laughter can release tension. It can remind us that we are more than the anger we feel. It can even bring people together over shared experiences.

Another lesser-known idea is the link between anger and personal boundaries. When we feel anger, it might be a sign that someone crossed a line. Maybe they took advantage of our kindness or invaded our privacy. In that sense, anger can guide us to strengthen our boundaries. We learn where we need to say no or set limits. Without anger, we might ignore such signs and allow repeated harm. That does not mean we lash out. It means we notice the signal and respond calmly but firmly. We clarify what we can accept and what we cannot. Over time, these boundaries help us feel safer. We reduce situations that provoke anger in the first place.

Transforming anger can be seen as a journey. We might start with explosive outbursts or silent resentment. We might then learn a few techniques to pause and breathe. We might practice better communication skills. We might reflect on old hurts that feed our anger. At times, we might slip back into old patterns. But each time, we can pick ourselves up and learn from the experience. Over months or years, we can see noticeable improvement. We feel more in control of our reactions. We handle disagreements with more poise. We still feel anger, but it no longer owns us. That progress can boost our confidence. It can also improve how others relate to us. As we become calmer, they might drop their defenses. They might be more willing to discuss issues openly. This can create a positive cycle of better communication for everyone involved.

Anger intersects with many facets of life. It shows up in politics, at home, in friendships, and even when we deal with strangers. If we master the art of transforming anger, we carry a valuable tool everywhere we go. We can be the ones who stay steady during heated debates. We can be the one who breaks the cycle of blame in a family argument. We can be the one who transforms frustration at a store clerk's mistake into a friendly conversation that resolves the problem. These small, daily examples might seem minor. But they add up. They create an atmosphere of respect and understanding. They also save us from the regret we feel after losing our temper. That regret can be a heavy burden. When we handle anger with grace, we avoid that weight.

There is a misconception that transforming anger means becoming passive. That is not true. We can still stand up for our rights without being aggressive. We can defend someone else who is wronged without hateful speech. We can be assertive and hold people accountable. The difference is that we do so from a place of clarity, not blind rage. This approach often yields better results. When we calmly state facts and remain respectful, people tend to listen more. Our arguments hold greater weight because they are not drowned in insults. This does not mean we will always get our way. But it does mean we behave with integrity. That integrity can inspire respect, even from those who disagree.

Sometimes, anger is tied to unmet needs. Perhaps we need more rest, more time with loved ones, or more recognition at work. If these needs go unspoken, frustration builds. Then a small event might trigger a big outburst. One helpful approach is to identify these needs early. We can express them directly rather than hoping others will guess. This prevents anger from swelling. It also fosters healthier connections, as people begin to communicate needs and boundaries more openly. Over time, this can reduce the stress that fuels anger. It also teaches self-awareness, which is vital for emotional balance.

Anger management does not mean we never feel angry again. That would be unrealistic. Anger, like all emotions, is part of being human. It will rise at times, especially in the face of injustice or hurt. The goal is to harness its energy. Instead of letting it rule us, we learn to guide it. That might involve practicing techniques like mindfulness, where we watch the anger as it grows, label it, and let it fade naturally. It might involve therapy if deep resentments or traumas lie behind our rage. It might involve group sessions where we share our stories and learn from others. Each path can contribute to the process of transformation. The important thing is recognizing that we have a choice. We do not have to be slaves to anger.

This journey can benefit from support. Friends, mentors, or mental health professionals can offer insights. They can observe patterns in us that we might miss. They can remind us that progress is possible when we feel discouraged. Sometimes, simply talking through a situation can reduce the anger we feel. We might find that naming our emotions out loud lightens their load. We might also gain ideas from people who overcame similar struggles. These connections remind us that we are not alone in dealing with anger. Many have walked this path and come out stronger on the other side.

In the end, transforming anger is about growth. It is about choosing a more constructive way to handle life's inevitable provocations. It is about breaking free from cycles of aggression or withdrawal. It is about preserving our health and nurturing our relationships. It allows us to stand up for what is right without trampling others. It helps us see the roots of our pain and address them in healthier ways. This transformation can bring a sense of relief as if a tight knot in our chest has loosened. It can bring more patience, compassion, and self-awareness. While anger will still arise, it will no longer dictate how we live. We become free to respond thoughtfully, guided by our values rather than raw emotion. That freedom can open many doors. It can lead to healing old wounds, building stronger bonds, and finding deeper peace within ourselves. This is the real power of transforming anger. It becomes not just an emotional improvement, but a path toward living with greater harmony and purpose.

10. Ego Unmasked

The word ego often brings to mind someone who brags or acts superior. Yet, ego runs deeper than bragging. It is the sense of "I" that we all carry. It shapes how we see ourselves. It also colors how we perceive others. Many people think of ego as pride, but it is more than that. The ego thrives on separation. It convinces us that we stand alone, distinct from everyone else. It says we must protect our status. It fears that if we fail, our worth vanishes. Because of this fear, ego can influence many decisions, often without our awareness. It whispers that we must always defend our position. It urges us to compete with others for recognition. It can make us chase praise, envy success, or hold grudges. By unmasking the ego, we can see its illusions and free ourselves from a cycle of insecurity. This freedom supports a more peaceful mind.

The ego tends to form when we are young. We begin to identify with certain labels. We might see ourselves as smart or as lacking talent. We might latch onto physical traits. We might compare ourselves to siblings or classmates. Over time, we piece together an image of who we are. That image includes our achievements, our likes and dislikes, and our social standing. It feels very real. But in truth, it is just a mental construct. It is a collection of stories and beliefs. Yet, ego insists that it is our core identity. It defends that identity fiercely. When someone questions part of it, we feel threatened. We might lash out or feel shame. The ego wants to prove it is correct. It wants to avoid any hint of being unimportant. This drive can cause stress and strain our relationships.

On the social level, ego can lead to many conflicts. People argue because they cannot stand to look weak. Leaders can start wars out of pride. Families can split when no one wants to be the first to apologize. Ego blocks empathy. It blocks the ability to see that someone else might have a point. It creates divides between groups who cling to

can improve if people let go of personal agendas. Creativity can flourish when no one tries to hog all the credit. Even in politics, leaders who are less driven by ego might serve their communities more sincerely. They might be willing to admit mistakes or collaborate across party lines. That said, it is no small task. The ego thrives in positions of power. It can blind leaders to the real needs of those they serve. Yet, the hope is that more individuals who see beyond ego can rise, inspiring a different model of leadership.

The importance of unmasking ego is linked to inner peace. The ego produces anxiety. It constantly compares and competes. It worries about how we look, and how we rank. It dreads losing respect. It can push us to chase endless external goals, leaving little room for rest. When we loosen the ego's hold, we free ourselves from that tension. We find that we can be content in the moment, whether praised or not. We still do our best, but our sense of worth no longer hinges on applause or success. This shift can lighten our hearts. It can also improve mental health. Many stress-related issues are traced back to fears about failure or status. By unmasking these ego-driven fears, we realize we are more resilient than we knew.

Another challenge is that the ego can be subtle. We might do a kind act and then feel a tug of pride. That pride by itself is not terrible. But if we dwell on it too long, we inflate our self-image. We start to think we are special compared to others. Then, if someone criticizes us, we might become defensive. We can learn to notice that wave of pride and let it pass. We can smile at the good deed and move on. We can also notice how our minds judge others automatically. Maybe we see a stranger and label them as less refined or less worthy. That is the ego asserting its rank. By catching these judgments, we can remind ourselves that each person has a life story. Each person has struggles and dreams. This small mental exercise chips away at the ego's habit of dividing us from them.

A lesser-known fact about ego is how it can influence group identities. Some of us take pride in belonging to certain groups: sports teams, religious communities, political parties, or nationalities. There is nothing wrong with feeling connection or loyalty. The danger is when this group identity becomes an extension of the ego. We might believe "our" group is superior. We might demonize others. Wars have been fueled by such group egos. Even in everyday life, this group ego can make us less open-minded. We may reject facts that challenge our tribe's stance. Unmasking ego in this context means seeing that belonging does not require blind pride. We can love our group while respecting others.

One method to unmask the ego is self-inquiry. We can sit quietly and ask, "Who am I?" We examine the thoughts that arise. We might say, "I am a mother, a student, an artist." But those are roles or labels. We might realize we are more than these roles. We might notice a deeper sense of being that is not defined by external identity. This can be an eye-opening process, though it might be unsettling at first. Another method is mindfulness. We pay attention to the present moment without judgment. When ego-based thoughts arise, we note them and let them go. Over time, we see how often we cling to stories about ourselves. We also realize we can step back from them. This space can bring relief. It does not erase personality. It just loosens our attachment to a fixed idea of who we must be.

The ego can also block genuine connections. When we are filled with self-importance, we do not truly hear others. Our mind is busy planning what to say next or how to boast. We miss the chance for real empathy. We remain stuck behind a wall of self-centered concerns. Conversely, by unmasking the ego, we become more present. We can give people our full attention. We sense their emotions. This deep listening fosters stronger bonds. It can heal rifts caused by misunderstanding. It also enriches our own life, as we discover the beauty of connecting at a heartfelt level. Many spiritual traditions teach that when the ego quiets, love flows more freely. This love is not just romantic or familial. It extends to all living beings. It recognizes a shared essence. That sense of oneness stands in stark contrast to the ego's isolation.

The journey of unmasking ego often meets resistance. Our minds cling to old habits. We might feel uneasy letting go of cherished identities. We might think, "If I am not my achievements, who am I?" Fear arises because we have invested so much in building that sense of self. But letting go does not mean losing everything. It means seeing that identity as fluid, not rigid. It means we can explore new aspects of ourselves. It means we can accept mistakes without feeling worthless. It also means we can let others shine without feeling diminished. The result can be surprising freedom.

Society benefits when more people unmask their egos. We see fewer power struggles in offices. We see more collaboration in community projects. We see less aggression on the roads, as drivers stop taking every slight personally. We might see more thoughtful dialogue in public forums, where participants focus on issues rather than defending personal pride. This is not a utopia. Human nature still has many layers. But each step toward less ego-driven behavior eases tension. It fosters trust. Children who grow up around less ego-driven adults learn healthier ways to express themselves. They become adults who do not rely on belittling others to feel strong.

An interesting aspect is how unmasking the ego can support creativity. Many artists fear negative feedback. Ego tells them that if their work is rejected, they are failures. This can lead to stress or avoidance of risk. But with a lighter ego, one might try bold ideas without being paralyzed by self-doubt. One might accept critiques as tools for improvement. This openness can lead to genuine breakthroughs. In the same way, unmasking ego can enhance leadership. A leader who is not blinded by ego can genuinely empower the team. They can delegate, listen to suggestions, and adapt strategies. The group becomes stronger because it draws from many minds, not just the leader's self-image.

There can be times when the ego tries to reassert itself. Suppose we have made progress in being humble. We might then feel pride in our humility. That is ego sneaking in the back door. We start to compare ourselves to those we deem less humble. We might feel a subtle superiority. This reveals how tricky the ego can be. The solution is to remain aware that unmasking the ego is a process, not a one-time achievement. We remain vigilant and laugh at ourselves when we catch the ego at work. That humor can dissolve tension. We realize we are all on a path of growth. No one is perfect or fully free from ego. But we can support each other in spotting it and releasing its grip.

Some lesser-known sources suggest that ego might be tied to survival instincts from our ancestors. When living in ancient conditions, protecting territory or status could be vital. But in modern life, these instincts can cause more harm than good. They make us overreact to harmless criticisms. They fuel office politics where real danger does not exist. By understanding that these impulses were once adaptive, we can forgive ourselves for them. Then we can choose to act differently because our current world often rewards cooperation more than aggression.

Unmasking the ego does not mean we become bland. Some fear they will lose their spark or drive. But a healthy sense of self can remain. We can still have dreams and passions. We can still celebrate accomplishments. We simply do not let those things define our entire being. We can be open to trying new hobbies without worrying about failing. We can let others share the spotlight. We can invest in relationships without using them for ego boosts. Life can become richer because our motivations expand beyond serving the self. We begin to ask how we can serve the greater good. That might mean volunteering, mentoring, or speaking out for justice. These actions gain depth when we do them without seeking applause.

Ego unmasked is not about becoming a saint. We will still have moments of vanity or envy. We will still want to protect our reputation at times. The difference is that we see these impulses as passing clouds. We do not let them dominate our behavior. When we slip, we can reflect and learn. Over time, we develop more compassion for ourselves and others. We see that everyone fights their own battle with ego. We grow less judgmental. We also experience a sense of unity. This unity can bring moments of peace. In those moments, we realize how connected we all are, beyond the labels and roles.

For many, spiritual practices help unmask the ego. Meditation, prayer, or chanting can quiet the mind enough to see beyond the noisy self. Others find that therapy or counseling sheds light on hidden ego-based fears. Still, others learn through life lessons: heartbreak, illness, or loss can shake the ego's foundation, revealing a deeper truth. Each path is valid. The common thread is a willingness to look within and question the stories we tell about ourselves. This questioning can be a gift. It can lead us toward greater self-knowledge and acceptance.

The social impact of unmasking the ego can be profound. Imagine a classroom where students do not bully or mock each other. Instead, they support classmates' strengths. They do not cling to being the best. They learn from each other. Imagine a neighborhood where people share resources without suspicion. They do not worry about who has a bigger house. They take pride in common well-being. These visions might seem distant, but they start with individuals. Each person who steps away from ego-driven competition brings a bit more harmony. Even small gestures, like letting someone speak without interruption, can ripple outward.

Ego unmasked shows us our humanity at its core. Without the ego's constant demands, we can experience simpler joys. We can appreciate nature, music, or a quiet moment without turning it into something about "me." We can be present for a friend in pain, giving our care freely. We can celebrate someone else's success as if it were our own. This openness fosters gratitude. Gratitude replaces the ego's sense of entitlement. We shift from "I deserve this" to "I am thankful for what

I have." That shift can free us from craving more and more. It can fill us with contentment.

This freedom from ego also enriches love. Romantic relationships can become calmer if we do not turn every disagreement into a battle for ego survival. We stop needing to be always right. We listen more. We see the person across from us as a partner, not a threat. Friendships blossom when we show genuine interest in others instead of waiting to talk about ourselves. Family gatherings lose some tension if members do not compete for attention or validation. Everywhere we look, unmasking ego brings space for kindness to flourish.

In the end, unmasking the ego supports a journey to inner peace. The ego stirs conflict, worry, and stress. When we begin to see it for what it is, we can laugh at our pretensions. We can notice how often we take things personally that were never about us. We can let others have their opinions without feeling attacked. We can respond rather than react. Day by day, we loosen the ego's grip. We feel lighter, and more at ease. We realize that behind all these roles and stories stands a deeper essence. That essence is calm, wise, and connected to all living beings. As we connect with that inner truth, we discover a wellspring of peace that does not depend on constant self-affirmation. This shift does not happen overnight. It unfolds with patience and practice. Yet, each small step brings new insights. We grow more tolerant, more curious, and more alive to the wonders around us. That growth is the priceless gift of unmasking the ego.

11. Facing Fear

Fear can creep into the mind at any moment. It can appear as a sudden chill when we face the unknown. It can tighten the chest and make us breathe faster. It can show up as a subtle unease when we have to speak our truth. Fear is natural, yet it can keep us from living fully. Many people struggle with it in different ways. Some fear failure. Others fear judgment. Some fear losing control. Still, others cannot even name the source of their anxiety. But fear is more than just a feeling. It can guide our decisions. It can shape our destinies if we let it. That is why learning to face fear can be a key step toward inner peace.

Facing fear does not mean we become fearless. It means we acknowledge that fear exists. It means we do not let it rule our lives. We feel the tremor but continue to act with courage. We accept that fear is a signal, not a dictator. This shift in perspective can reduce the hold fear has over us. Yet, it can be easier said than done. Many people avoid scary situations and think that is the solution. They assume that if they never step outside their comfort zone, fear will vanish. In reality, it often grows in hidden ways. We might gain temporary relief, but the fear can lurk in the shadows. It can still limit our choices.

Fear can affect society in many areas. When groups of people feel scared, tensions can rise. They might isolate themselves from those they view as different. They might pass laws that close borders or restrict freedoms. They might blame specific communities for their problems. In this way, fear can lead to bigotry or conflicts that harm everyone. Fear can also hold back innovation. If companies or organizations fear failure too much, they might not explore bold ideas. They might stay stuck in old patterns. This slows progress. It can also cause boredom and frustration for those who want change. In families, fear can strain relationships. Parents might fear letting children take risks, so they overprotect them. That can stunt children's growth. Siblings might fear losing favor, so they compete harshly. Partners might fear abandonment, so they cling or push each other away. These patterns can create tension and sadness.

It is important to face fear because it unlocks new possibilities. When we challenge our worries, we often find they are less powerful than we imagined. We learn that we can handle outcomes that once seemed unbearable. We see that we are stronger or more adaptable than we believe. This discovery can spark personal growth. It can widen our perspective. We become more open to trying fresh experiences. We stop feeling stuck. We also relate to others more calmly. If we are not ruled by fear, we are less reactive. We can listen instead of jumping to defend ourselves. That can improve cooperation and empathy. When entire groups shift in that manner, communities become more harmonious. Dialogues become less heated. People begin to trust each other more.

There are many challenges on the path to facing fear. One is the comfort zone. It might be limiting, but it feels safe. We have routines and habits that do not threaten our sense of control. Stepping out of that zone can feel alarming. Another challenge is a lack of support. If our close friends or family do not encourage us, we might give up. We might also face harsh judgments from people who do not understand our journey. Also, some fears are deeply rooted in past trauma. That makes them more complex. A single pep talk might not be enough. We may need therapy or guidance to unravel old wounds. Another challenge is that fear can wear many masks. We might not even recognize it. It might show anger, perfectionism, or procrastination. Unless we look beneath the surface, we might not see the fear driving these behaviors.

Despite these obstacles, many people have found ways to deal with fear. One lesser-known fact is that fear has a cycle. The body and mind detect a threat, and then adrenaline surges. We tense up, our hearts pound, and we feel that urge to flee or fight. However, if we ride out that wave, the intense reaction often subsides within a few minutes. This is especially true in situations that do not involve actual danger.

Another interesting fact is that fear can trick us into believing the worst outcomes will occur. Psychologists call this catastrophic thinking. Our minds leap to the most extreme scenario. Yet, real life often falls somewhere in the middle. Learning to recognize these mental exaggerations can help us challenge them. Over time, we become less startled by them.

Facing fear offers many rewards, starting with self-discovery. We learn about what triggers us and why. We see parts of ourselves that remain hidden under worry or denial. We might realize that we hold untapped skills. We might discover a deeper resilience. We also gain empathy for others who battle similar fears. This empathy can inspire us to reach out, to support friends who feel anxious. As we share our experiences, we break the isolation that fear can cause. Another reward is a sense of freedom. Each time we face a fear, we reclaim some power. We show ourselves that we are not confined by our anxieties. This can lead to a lasting boost in confidence. Even if we do not succeed in every attempt, the act of trying becomes a victory. We grow from the process, no matter the result.

Socially, people who face fear may become role models. They set an example that courage is possible. They encourage others to do the same. We often admire those who stand up against injustice or personal limitations. These figures teach us that fear does not have to win. They remind us that small acts of bravery can build over time. Eventually, they lead to big changes. Even a quiet person who conquers stage fright by giving a speech can inspire others. It shows that ordinary individuals can do impressive things once they step through fear's gate.

There are many techniques for facing fear. One common method is gradual exposure. We approach what scares us in small steps. If someone fears public speaking, they might start by speaking in front of a friend. Then they might move to a small group. Over time, they tackle bigger audiences. Another helpful tool is visualization. We imagine ourselves handling the fear calmly. We see ourselves succeeding or at least staying composed. That mental rehearsal can reduce anxiety when we face a real situation. Breathing exercises also help. Slow, deep breaths calm the nervous system. They signal the brain that we are safe. Instead of shallow, rapid breathing, which fuels panic, we choose a measured pace. This can ground us in the moment.

Certain people find mindfulness valuable. By focusing on the present, they keep the mind from spinning out of control. Fear often grows from what might happen, not what is happening right now. By observing our thoughts without clinging to them, we weaken fear's grip. Another approach is seeking knowledge. Many fears thrive on the unknown. If we learn about the thing we fear, we see it more objectively. We realize that some dangers are less likely than we thought. This can apply to things like flying or traveling alone. Data and facts can ease baseless worries.

However, not all fear is irrational. Sometimes we do face real threats. In these cases, facing fear might involve wise caution. If we fear reckless driving, that is valid. We can still address it by adopting safe driving habits. Or if we fear heights, perhaps we train with experts who teach us about gear and technique for climbing. Facing fear does not mean ignoring risk. It means acknowledging it and preparing ourselves. It means we do not let the fear paralyze us. Instead, we learn to navigate the situation with knowledge and skill.

Fear can also have a strange way of pushing us toward growth. Some individuals find that a surge of fear forced them to question their path. For instance, fear of speaking in public might lead someone to explore new methods of communication. They might discover a talent for writing or leading small group discussions. Fear can nudge us to explore corners of life we might have missed. We may initially wish to avoid it. But by leaning in, we discover opportunities. This is not about romanticizing fear. It is about recognizing that fear sometimes shines a light on what we most need to address.

The social importance of fear management is huge. Imagine a workplace where everyone can speak up without fear of ridicule. That environment tends to be more innovative. Problems are solved faster because people share ideas. Or think about a community where people do not fear those who come from different backgrounds. They learn from one another. They cooperate to solve common issues. Fear of the unknown can stand in the way of such unity. But if we face it, we open doors to rich cultural exchange. On a larger scale, fear of conflict can lead nations to avoid dialogue. They might prefer isolation. Yet, if leaders face their fear of negotiation, they might find peaceful solutions. This can prevent wars. This shows how fear can shape history.

One challenge that arises is that many industries profit from fear. Some media outlets highlight frightening stories to grab attention. Viewers tune in, their fears stoked. Over time, this can create a culture of anxiety. People see threats everywhere. This fear can push them to buy products or services that promise safety. In politics, fear can be used to sway public opinion. Candidates might claim that an outside group is dangerous. They promise protection if elected. This tactic can win votes, but it also fosters division. That is why being aware of how fear is used around us is vital. When we face fear consciously, we can see through manipulations. We do not let those messages control us so easily.

There are lesser-known facts about the biology of fear. The amygdala in the brain plays a big role. It processes emotional responses, especially to threats. When we feel fear, the amygdala signals the release of hormones. Our heart rate goes up. Blood moves away from digestion and into muscles. That is a holdover from when humans needed to fight predators. Now, we rarely face a saber-toothed tiger, yet the response remains. Our modern world triggers that ancient system in new ways. For instance, hearing an unexpected noise at night can set off the same chain reaction. This knowledge helps us see fear as normal, not as a flaw.

It reminds us that the body is trying to protect us, even if it misreads certain cues.

Facing fear can also improve our mental health overall. Anxiety disorders often involve a heightened sense of fear or worry. By learning to face fear in small steps, people can reduce general anxiety. They realize that many concerns do not materialize. Or if they do, they are not as awful as imagined. This exposure approach is a known therapy technique. It takes patience, but the results can be life-changing. People become more functional in daily activities. Their relationships improve as they take part in normal social events instead of hiding away.

Fear also ties to creativity. Many artists speak of a fear that holds them back from fully expressing themselves. They might worry about critics or about failing to create something good. Some get stuck in perfectionism. But when they face that fear, they open a door to experimentation. They allow themselves to produce imperfect drafts. From those drafts come discoveries. Similarly, in entrepreneurship, fear of failure can stop someone from starting a business. If they confront that fear, they might begin a project that transforms their life. Not every venture succeeds. But even in failure, lessons arise. These lessons shape future endeavors. Without facing fear, we remain in place, wondering what might have been.

It helps to remember that fear is universal. Every culture has myths about bravery and terror. Humans have always told stories to cope with the unknown. We see old rituals to appease spirits or to protect villages from curses. These show that fear is deeply woven into our collective psyche. Yet, we have also developed traditions of courage, from warrior rites to spiritual pilgrimages. Today, we can draw wisdom from many sources. We see that fear can bond us if we share our vulnerabilities. We also see that different cultures approach fear in creative ways, such as through festivals that mock scary figures. Recognizing the common thread of fear around the globe can foster compassion. We understand that we are not alone in feeling frightened at times.

A big question arises: how can we apply these ideas in daily life? We can start by naming our fear when it appears. That simple act can weaken its grip. Instead of saying, "I can't do this," we say, "I feel scared about this." We shift the focus from a rigid belief to a passing emotion. Then we can ask, "What is the cause?" We might find hidden worries like, "I fear being embarrassed if I fail." Next, we can explore how realistic that worry is. We might see that even if we fail, we can handle the outcome. That clarity can give us courage. Then we take small steps. We do not expect ourselves to leap over the fear in one go. We practice in safe environments. We celebrate small wins. If we face setbacks, we treat them as lessons.

Support from others can be priceless. A friend's encouragement might nudge us beyond our hesitation. A mentor's advice can reassure us. A shared experience can show that we are not alone. If fear is overwhelming, professional help is an option. Therapists can guide us through structured methods. They can tailor approaches to our specific fears. This can be especially helpful if trauma is involved. Some people also turn to faith or spiritual guidance. They trust in a higher force or cosmic perspective, which makes fears seem smaller. The important thing is to find a path that resonates with us. We do not need to walk alone.

When we grow more comfortable with facing fear, we often notice a shift in how we see challenges. Obstacles become less intimidating. We view them as puzzles rather than threats. We become more willing to try new things. We might join a club, learn a skill, or travel abroad. We see that even if fear pops up, we know how to handle it. That knowledge builds inner peace. We no longer feel at the mercy of our anxieties. We become co-creators of our future. This does not mean fear disappears forever. It still visits from time to time. But we meet it with a sense of familiarity. We say, "I know you. Let's figure this out together." That approach transforms fear from an enemy into a teacher.

The social impact of this transformation can be powerful. Families that share honest conversations about fear can foster resilience in children. Schools that encourage healthy risk-taking can produce creative thinkers. Communities that tackle shared fears can solve problems more effectively. They can address crime or health issues without falling into panic. Even on a global level, cooperative efforts require courage. If we fear losing an advantage, we might refuse to collaborate. But if we face that fear, we can build alliances. We can work on global challenges like climate change or inequality in a spirit of shared responsibility.

People who walk the path of facing fear often speak of a newfound zest for life. They describe feeling awake in ways they never did before. They become grateful for small joys because they no longer waste energy dreading the future. Some mention a deeper sense of connection to others. They realize that many are just as scared. They see that behind anger or aloofness can lie fear. This insight fosters compassion. It helps defuse conflict. It can also spark a desire to help others overcome their fears. That desire can lead to supportive communities or volunteer work. In these spaces, people lift each other.

It is essential to remember that facing fear is an ongoing process. We do not conquer fear once and for all. Life brings new challenges. Our minds can conjure new anxieties. But each time we tackle one fear, we gain a skill set. We become more adaptable. We learn that we can survive discomfort. We learn that we can pivot if things go wrong. That knowledge stays with us. It becomes part of our inner strength. So, when the next fear arises, we are less shaken. We might still feel it, but we say, "I've been through worse. I'll manage." This pattern can continue throughout our days, shaping us into more resilient individuals.

Sometimes, people worry that living without fear means living recklessly. They think that if we do not fear danger, we will behave foolishly. But healthy caution is not the same as paralyzing fear. There is a place for prudent assessment. We can weigh the risks and benefits. We can choose safe practices without letting fear cripple us. Fear was meant to signal caution, not to shut us down. By facing it, we re-establish that balance. We use caution as a tool, not as a chain. We do not let it block opportunities that might enrich our lives. We remain mindful but open.

Facing fear also ties to self-worth. Sometimes fear arises because we doubt our ability to cope with disappointment. We think that if we fail, it means we are unlovable. By challenging that assumption, we see that our worth does not hinge on success or failure. We remain worthy and human, regardless of the outcome. This realization can melt away much of the fear related to performance. It lets us approach tasks with curiosity. We become free to explore. We might even find that the journey matters more than the destination. Fear often tries to bully us into believing we must protect ourselves from any risk to our self-image. But once we see that we are inherently valuable, fear's threats hold less weight.

Many spiritual paths emphasize facing fear with acceptance. They teach that resisting fear only gives it more energy. Instead, we observe it with compassion. We see it as a wave passing through. We do not try to block it. We also do not let it carry us away. We stay present, breathing through the sensations. This practice can lead to a profound sense of peace. It is not always easy. Our instincts might scream to escape the feeling. But if we stay, we learn that the wave eventually dissolves. We remain, grounded and intact. This approach is common in mindfulness and meditation circles. Yet, one does not need to be spiritual to try it. It is a universal technique.

In summary, facing fear is a journey that affects every corner of life. It shapes how we see ourselves, how we interact with others, and how we tackle challenges. It can transform entire families or communities. It is not a quick fix, nor is it about never feeling scared again. It is about understanding fear's nature, its triggers, and its illusions. It is about choosing to move forward even with trembling hands. It is about respecting real dangers while refusing to bow to imaginary ones. It is about discovering that courage grows from small steps. It is about reclaiming our power each time we dare to act despite fear. Over time, these steps accumulate into a life of greater freedom and peace. That is why facing fear holds such importance on the path to inner harmony. It unlocks doors we might never have known existed. It shows us that our limits are often mental barriers, waiting to be crossed. Once we see that, the future opens up in ways both subtle and grand. We find that we are capable of far more than we believed. And in that realization, we touch the quiet strength that resides within us all.

12. Letting Go

Letting go can feel both painful and freeing. It often involves releasing what we thought we could not live without. It might be the end of a relationship, the loss of a job, or the fading of an old dream. Sometimes, it is a subtle shift inside us. We realize we have been clinging to beliefs or habits that no longer serve us. Other times, it is an abrupt change, like a sudden move to a new city. Letting go is rarely simple. It can shake our sense of security. Yet, on the other side of this process, there can be peace. We discover that life does not collapse when we release our tight grip. It can open in ways we never expected.

For many, the act of letting go seems risky. We assume that if we loosen our hold on something, we will lose control. We worry that life will spin out of balance. We fear that we will make ourselves vulnerable to pain. Yet, holding on too tightly can create another kind of suffering. We become tense, defensive, or stuck in the past. We miss new possibilities because we refuse to release old attachments. Letting go is not about giving up or being lazy. It is about recognizing that certain things are beyond our control or no longer in our best interest. It involves trust—in ourselves, in others, and the unfolding of events.

Sometimes, letting go means accepting that a situation cannot be forced. We might strive to fix or improve something beyond our power. If we refuse to let go, frustration grows. We might push harder, ignoring signals that our efforts are not fruitful. This can strain our relationships and our well-being. However, if we pause and admit that we have done what we can, we might find relief. This relief does not mean everything is solved. It only means we have allowed life to move forward without our constant pressure. That moment of acceptance can be profound. It can free our energy for new choices.

Letting go has social implications as well. Imagine a community that cannot let go of old grudges. Conflicts remain alive for decades. Groups define themselves by historical resentments. Progress stalls because no one forgives or forgets. On the other hand, if individuals learn to let go of past wrongs, they can form fresh bonds. They can cooperate for the common good. This does not mean ignoring justice or ignoring lessons from mistakes. It means releasing the desire to stay stuck in anger or blame. In this sense, letting go fosters harmony. It can open space for dialogue and healing, whether in families, workplaces, or entire societies.

It is important to consider how letting go affects personal well-being. People who cling to regrets or guilt can carry emotional burdens for years. They replay old scenarios and wonder how they could have done better. They remain trapped in a mental loop. By letting go of self-blame, they can learn from mistakes more healthily. They can direct their attention to new goals or ways to grow. Similarly, those who hold onto heartbreak might struggle to open up to new love. They fear repeating pain or betrayal. But letting go of that fear can allow them to trust again. It might lead to deeper connections in the future. This aspect of letting go is crucial for emotional health. It helps us move forward instead of dwelling on what was lost.

Challenges arise when we try to let go. One challenge is the belief that letting go equals failure. We think we must keep fighting for something, even if it no longer aligns with our values or well-being. We mix up persistence with stubbornness. Another challenge is nostalgia. We recall the past in a rosy light, forgetting the real issues. This selective memory can keep us tied to illusions. Also, fear of the unknown can block us. Letting go can mean stepping into a void. We do not know what will replace what we release. That uncertainty can be frightening. Yet, often that open space invites new growth. Overcoming these challenges can require inner work and patience. It can demand that we trust a process we do not fully understand.

Many people do not realize how letting go can link to creativity. Sometimes, we hold onto old methods or opinions so tightly that we block fresh ideas. By letting go of fixed mindsets, we allow unexpected solutions to appear. Artists, writers, and scientists often discover breakthroughs when they abandon a rigid approach. They experiment, fail, and try a new angle. This open-mindedness is a form of letting go. It says, "I release the need to be right or perfect. I will explore possibilities." The same principle can apply to everyday life. By letting go of the demand that life proceed exactly as we planned, we open ourselves to creative ways of living. We can adapt to changes rather than fight them.

Letting go also has some lesser-known physical effects. Chronic stress can come from clinging to worries or resentments. The body reacts with tense muscles, poor sleep, or digestive problems. When we learn to let go of persistent tension or negative thoughts, stress hormones may decrease. We might breathe more freely. Our immune system can function better. These improvements might seem small, but they can add up to better overall health. Sometimes, people who practice letting go regularly, such as through meditation or therapy, report feeling lighter or more energetic. They notice that old aches fade. Although this does not replace medical care, it shows how the mind and body connect.

On a more spiritual level, many traditions speak of the power of letting go. In some teachings, it is called surrender. Not surrender to an enemy, but surrender to life's greater flow. It means releasing the ego's insistence on controlling everything. This is not about giving up our basic responsibilities. It is about recognizing that we are part of a bigger whole. We cannot micromanage all outcomes. By surrendering, we align ourselves with a sense of peace or trust in a higher wisdom. This might sound lofty, yet it can manifest in small daily acts. For example, we might pause before reacting to a conflict and choose to let go of the urge to argue. Or we might relinquish a planned route on a trip when faced with a blocked road, allowing ourselves to discover a new path. These small surrenders can nurture a calm and flexible outlook.

Letting go can be especially important when dealing with grief or loss. Whether it is the death of a loved one, the end of a relationship, or the loss of a job, the pain can be intense. Holding onto what is gone can prolong that pain. We might replay every memory, clinging to what used to be. While it is healthy to grieve, at some point we must let go of the past as our only focus. This does not mean forgetting or dismissing what happened. It means making space for the present. We honor what was, then gradually return to life's flow. Over time, letting go can help us integrate the loss into a broader story. We carry the memories gently, without letting them chain us to sorrow. This process can take time, especially with deep losses. Patience and self-compassion are vital.

Social media sometimes makes letting go harder. People see reminders of past connections or experiences. They might see photos of an ex-partner or read updates about a job they left. This can stir up old emotions. It can tempt them to dwell on regrets or envy. One approach is to set boundaries with digital tools. That might include unfollowing accounts that trigger painful thoughts or limiting time online. Another approach is to face those triggers more mindfully. Each time the old feeling arises, they practice letting it go again. This can feel repetitive, but it builds emotional strength.

Letting go also matters in conflicts between nations or communities. History is full of grudges that lasted centuries. People define themselves by ancient battles or wrongs. That cycle can keep hatred alive through multiple generations. Letting go on a cultural level does not mean denying the past. It means choosing not to keep hatred burning. It can involve efforts to repair relationships, to acknowledge pain, and to find ways to coexist. When enough individuals in a community practice letting go of vengeance or prejudice, a door to peace can open. The process is complex. It might demand real accountability and genuine apologies. But it also requires the willingness to release the identity of being an eternal victim or aggressor. That is a profound letting go.

One might wonder how to start letting go in daily life. The first step is awareness. We notice when we are holding on too tightly to something, such as a rigid plan or a certain image of ourselves. We name it: "I am clinging to the idea that I must succeed at all costs." Then we explore why. Perhaps we fear failure or shame. Maybe we attach our self-worth to that success. Once we see the root, we can challenge it. We can ask, "What if I let go of this demand? Would I still be okay?" Often, we realize we would survive. The tension eases. Another step is to practice letting go in small, safe ways. We might start with a tiny disappointment, like a canceled meeting. We let ourselves adapt, and we notice that life goes on. Over time, these small moments build our capacity for bigger releases.

Some people find rituals helpful. They might write down what they wish to let go of, then tear up the paper. They might speak out loud, "I release this fear," or "I let go of this anger." Symbolic acts can imprint the intention on the mind. Also, certain physical practices like yoga or mindful exercise can teach the body to release tension, which can mirror emotional release. Talking to a trusted friend or counselor can also help. They might offer a perspective that keeps us from falling back into the same mental loops. There is no single right way to let go. Each person must find what resonates with them.

There is an interesting link between letting go and forgiveness. When we hold grudges, we carry the weight of anger or hurt. By letting go, we free ourselves from that burden. Forgiving does not mean we say the harm was acceptable. It means we refuse to remain chained to the pain. In some cases, we might never receive an apology, or the other person might be gone. Still, we can choose to let go within ourselves. This choice can be deeply healing. It does not have to involve reconciliation or contact. It is more about releasing the grip that old events have on our hearts. Over time, this can restore our ability to trust and connect. That, in turn, can enhance our sense of peace.

Letting go can also apply to success. Many of us chase achievements in work, sports, or creative fields. We become so attached to the idea of winning that we lose sight of the present. We measure our worth by results. This can breed anxiety and even sabotage our performance. By letting go of the outcome, we become more focused on the process. We practice or perform with full attention, not with the frantic thought, "I must win." Ironically, this calmer approach often leads to better performance. We operate from a place of flow rather than tension. If the outcome is not what we hoped, we recover more quickly. We do not see it as a total failure. We see it as part of growth. This mindset can liberate us from the constant pressure to prove ourselves.

Some people think letting go means losing ambition or passion. That is a misconception. We can still have goals and drive. The difference is that we hold them with openness. We do not define our entire identity by them. We allow life to shift and reveal other paths. We do our best, but we do not cling to one specific version of the future. That attitude can reduce stress and spark creativity. It can also make us more adaptable when circumstances change. The world is full of surprises, and letting go of rigid plans can help us move with life's currents rather than fighting them.

Social gatherings can highlight the need for letting go. We might attend events with the desire to control every detail. We want others to behave in certain ways. We want conversations to go smoothly. If reality does not match our plan, frustration bubbles up. But by letting go of those expectations, we can simply be present. We can engage with what is, not with what we wish it to be. This can make gatherings more relaxed. We might discover that spontaneous moments are the most delightful. The same principle applies to traveling. If we cling to a strict itinerary, we might miss local wonders or new friends. Letting go lets us see hidden gems.

Another area where letting go matters is when children grow up. Parents can find it hard to release control. They might cling to the idea of always being needed. But children must step into their independence. If parents refuse to let go, conflicts arise. By letting go gradually, parents show trust in their children's ability to navigate life. This can foster confidence on both sides. The same dynamic can show up in romantic or platonic relationships. Clinging can choke affection. Letting each person breathe can strengthen the bond. When we trust the connection, we do not need to hold it in a vice grip.

At times, letting go can mean leaving behind a dream. Maybe we realize that a lifelong goal no longer fits who we are. We might feel guilt or confusion. We invested so much time. Yet, letting go can open space for a new dream that aligns with our current self. This does not dismiss our past efforts. They shaped us. But we accept that we have evolved. We move on without bitterness. This can be a sign of maturity, acknowledging that life is not static. The ability to shift direction can lead to unexpected fulfillment.

Letting go also applies to identity. Some people cling to roles like "the funny one" or "the successful one." They fear that without that label, they lose all sense of self. But identity can be fluid. We can explore new facets of personality. We can try different hobbies or relate to people in new ways. This might bring surprising joy. Holding onto a rigid identity can limit personal evolution. By letting go of old definitions, we allow ourselves to grow. That growth can lead to deeper self-knowledge and more fulfilling relationships.

A lesser-known fact about letting go is how it can reduce anxiety about the future. We often worry about events that might happen. We try to plan and control everything. But life remains uncertain. By letting go of the illusion of total control, we can find calm. We focus on what we can do now. We understand that the future will have unknown elements. This perspective fosters resilience. We know we can adapt. We also realize that sometimes, the future might bring pleasant surprises. If we cling to a single outcome, we miss those better paths that appear.

We can see how letting go relates to many other themes, like forgiveness, patience, gratitude, and kindness. When we let go of resentment, we forgive. When we let go of impatience, we learn to wait. When we let go of complaints, we grow more grateful for what we have. When we let go of judgment, we become kinder to others. Each form of release lightens the weight on our hearts. This is why letting go stands as a cornerstone in many guides to inner peace. It underlies so many emotional skills. Without it, we remain trapped in cycles of tension or negativity.

If we still doubt the power of letting go, we can try a small experiment. Picture a clenched fist. Imagine you hold sand inside. If you tighten your grip, the sand slips out. You lose most of it. But if you hold your palm open, the sand rests gently. You keep it without force. Letting go works similarly in life. When we cling too tightly, we can damage what we hold. When we loosen up, we can appreciate it more fully, while also allowing for change. That is the paradox: by letting go, we can experience deeper bonds, healthier love, and more meaningful achievements.

In the end, letting go is not about shutting ourselves off. It is about staying in the present and accepting that change is natural. It is about honoring what was, yet making space for what is to come. This shift can happen gently or suddenly, depending on circumstances. But the result is often a sense of relief and expanded perspective. People who cultivate this skill report feeling lighter inside. They find themselves more flexible, less stressed, and better able to connect with others. Letting go does not fix every problem. However, it lays a foundation for growth, healing, and discovery. It invites us to live more freely, with open hands and an open heart. And that may be one of the greatest gifts on the path to inner peace.

13. Releasing Regret

Releasing regret can bring a profound sense of relief. Many people carry regret for years, wishing they had chosen differently or spoken other words. Sometimes, regret grows quietly in the mind, like a small thorn that pricks whenever certain memories appear. Other times, it roars like a storm, flooding thoughts day and night. This feeling can arise from lost opportunities, unkind actions, or words left unsaid. It can revolve around career choices, romances, or even friendships that drifted away. No matter the cause, regret often leads to deep sorrow. It can weigh us down and stop us from living in the present. Yet, when we learn to release regret, we may find new energy and hope. We understand that life can still hold joy, even after mistakes or missed chances. This process of releasing regret can transform our outlook and free us from chains we did not realize we were carrying.

Regret can have a social impact beyond the personal sphere. A person filled with regret might withdraw from others. They could feel too guilty or embarrassed to engage fully. This can strain relationships, as friends or family might sense the distance but not understand the cause. In some cases, regret over harming someone can make a person overly cautious. They might avoid forming new bonds to ensure they never repeat the same error. Over time, this may lead to isolation. On a larger scale, communities can also suffer from collective regrets. A group might lament past decisions or actions that caused harm. If they do not address these regrets openly, tension can linger for years. This can hinder cooperation, as members remain stuck in blame. Releasing regret, in this context, can pave the way for healing. It allows a group to acknowledge what went wrong and then move forward with lessons learned. It does not erase history, but it eases old bitterness.

The importance of releasing regret also appears in mental and emotional health. Regret can be a quiet poison, draining confidence and creating stress. It often hides behind sadness or anger. Some people try to bury regret with distractions, hoping it will fade. Yet, that can lead to other issues like addiction or chronic anxiety. The more we push regret away, the more it might solidify. This is why facing regret can be an act of courage. When we turn to it, we begin to unravel the tangled emotions. We see that, yes, we might have made errors or allowed chances to slip by. But these are part of being human. No one sails through life without mistakes. Once we accept this, we can start to release the shame. We can allow ourselves the space to move on with wisdom gained from our experiences. That new freedom can improve mood, strengthen relationships, and inspire personal growth.

Challenges arise when we attempt to release regret. One hurdle is our judgment. We might think we "should have known better." We might label ourselves as failures. This self-condemnation can tighten the grip of regret. Another challenge is the fear that letting go of regret means dismissing its lessons. In truth, releasing regret does not mean we forget what happened. It means we stop punishing ourselves. We can still keep the insights we gained. Another challenge is that regret can become familiar, almost a twisted form of comfort. We replay the past in our minds, wishing to rewrite it. That loop can feel safer than stepping into the unknown future. Letting go demands stepping away from that cycle. That can feel scary at first, even though it is ultimately liberating.

Regret can even shape entire family dynamics. Parents might regret not spending enough time with their children. Children might regret not appreciating their parents while they were alive. Siblings might regret harsh words exchanged long ago. These regrets can linger like shadows, affecting how family members interact. If no one addresses them, they can sour every gathering. On the other hand, if someone decides to break the pattern, it can bring healing. They might start an honest conversation, acknowledging the pain. That conversation can end years of quiet tension. It can also set an example for younger relatives about the power of facing regret. This kind of release might require patience and understanding. It might not solve every issue overnight, but it can reduce a burden that has weighed on everyone for too long.

One lesser-known fact is that regret can sometimes inspire positive change. A person who regrets not pursuing a dream might decide to take classes or start a new project. They transform their remorse into motivation. Similarly, a leader who regrets a poor decision might strive to become more thoughtful, improving future outcomes. In these cases, regret becomes a signal rather than a prison. It tells us something is not right, and we can choose to respond constructively. This shift from destructive guilt to purposeful action often marks a key step in releasing regret. We do not stay stuck in shame. We use regret's energy to move forward.

Social media can intensify regret in modern life. People see images of others living perfect lives, traveling, or achieving milestones. Someone might regret not living that life. They compare themselves and feel they fell behind. But much of what we see online is curated. It rarely shows the full story. Those who appear to have no regrets might carry silent burdens. Recognizing the illusions of social media can help reduce envy and the regrets tied to unrealistic comparisons. In truth, everyone has regrets of some sort, even if they never share them publicly. Accepting this fact can ease the pressure and remind us that we are not alone in our struggles.

Regret sometimes shows up as constant "what if" thoughts. We imagine different outcomes if we had chosen another path. We might think, "What if I had said yes to that job?" or "What if I had been braver in telling someone I loved them?" These daydreams can be bittersweet. They provide a fantasy of what might have been. Yet, they can also keep us from seeing the good in our real situation. While it is okay to reflect, too much time stuck in hypothetical scenarios can sap our energy. We might neglect the present, which is the only place we can truly act. A more balanced approach is to catch ourselves in "what if" thinking and gently bring focus back to what we can do now. That might be as simple as a small step toward a new goal or an act of kindness that reopens a lost friendship.

Releasing regret can also involve forgiving others. Perhaps someone else contributed to our missed opportunity or mistake. We might blame them for giving poor advice or for betraying our trust. If we cling to that anger, regret mingles with resentment, creating a heavier emotional load. Forgiving them does not mean approving what they did. It means we stop letting their actions dominate our thoughts. We decide to move on without bearing that grudge. This can be challenging, especially if the hurt is deep. Still, forgiveness can lighten our spirit. It can also free us from the desire for revenge, which rarely leads to true healing. Over time, this release can open new paths, either for reconciliation or for peacefully parting ways.

Many people who struggle with regret also wrestle with perfectionism. They think they should have done everything flawlessly. They hold themselves to an impossible standard. When life does not match that standard, regret sets in. Part of releasing regret means accepting our humanity. We all have limited knowledge at any given time. We make choices based on who we are and what we know then. Later, we might see better options. But that does not negate the fact that we did our best in that moment. Easing the grip of perfectionism can reduce regret. We start to see each step as part of a journey. Sometimes we stumble, yet each stumble can lead to deeper insight.

Interestingly, regret can also appear in cases of success. Someone might achieve a big goal but regret the path they took. Maybe they neglected loved ones or compromised values. They might carry guilt. They wonder if the outcome was worth the cost. Releasing this regret could involve making amends or changing future behavior. Perhaps they decide to spend more time with family now or to use their success to help others. In this sense, regret can guide us to realign with our core principles. It prompts us to ask, "Is this path truly right for me?" That question can open new horizons.

Sometimes, regret sits like a heavy knot in the heart, especially when we cannot apologize to a person we hurt. Maybe they are gone, or they do not wish to speak with us. This can feel deeply painful. In such situations, releasing regret might involve a symbolic act. We can write a letter to them, expressing our sorrow, even if we never send it. We can reflect on how we might treat others better moving forward. We can also honor that person's memory in a meaningful way, perhaps by volunteering or dedicating a small act of service in their name. These gestures can bring a sense of closure, even if it is incomplete. Over time, we can learn to hold compassion for ourselves as well, acknowledging that we have grown since then.

Many spiritual traditions address regret as part of the human experience. Some call it repentance or confession. Others emphasize the need to reconcile with the past to find inner peace. They often suggest that regret alone does not serve unless it leads to change or understanding. The true release comes when we integrate lessons and move on. This echoes in secular circles too, through therapy or self-help approaches. The common thread is that regret, when properly addressed, can evolve into insight. That insight, in turn, can spark personal transformation. We do not need to remain stuck in self-blame or sadness. We can channel regret into a deeper compassion for ourselves and others.

Releasing regret can also enhance mental clarity. When we stop clinging to old stories, our minds open to fresh possibilities. This clarity might encourage us to try new ventures or relationships without the burden of guilt. We feel less defined by what went wrong and more curious about what could go right. This can boost creativity and problem-solving. It can also lift the mood. People weighed down by regret often feel powerless. But once they start letting it go, they regain a sense of agency. They see that each day offers choices. Their past does not chain them completely. In that shift, hope appears where despair once stood.

Certain lesser-known techniques can help in releasing regret. One is the use of mindful awareness. We sit quietly and notice regretful thoughts without judging them. We might label them as "regret" and watch them drift by. Over time, they lose power. Another approach is to reframe the story we tell about our past. Instead of calling ourselves foolish, we describe ourselves as learners on a path. We highlight what we gained instead of only what we lost. This shift in narrative can gradually change how we feel. Also, some find it helpful to share regrets in a supportive group. Hearing others' stories can lessen isolation. We see that regret is not a personal failing but a universal condition. That comfort can ease shame.

Socially, as more people learn to release regret, communities might become more forgiving. They might adopt restorative practices for those who made mistakes. Instead of shunning them forever, they might encourage amends and second chances. This can have far-reaching effects. Recidivism rates might drop if individuals are not burdened by endless guilt or societal rejection. Families could mend. Workplaces might allow employees to learn from errors rather than punishing them harshly. This cultural shift would not excuse bad behavior. It would simply acknowledge that growth is possible after a lapse. It would also reduce the heavy toll that long-term regret can inflict on mental health.

Releasing regret ties closely to self-worth. Some regrets arise because we believe we do not deserve forgiveness. We might feel worthless due to our mistakes. We might sabotage new opportunities, thinking we are doomed to fail again. This cycle feeds on regret. However, if we begin to see ourselves as redeemable, regret can loosen its grip. We realize we are more than our errors. We can treat ourselves with kindness, offering the same compassion we would extend to a friend. This process can be slow and may require guidance, but it can open a path to true self-acceptance. Over time, we stop viewing ourselves solely through the lens of regret and start seeing the full picture of who we are.

Regret can also be tied to cultural norms. In certain cultures, there might be a strong emphasis on honor or family duty. A small mistake could feel monumental, leading to intense regret. People might believe they brought shame to the entire family. Releasing regret in such contexts can be tricky. It may involve conversations with elders or community leaders. It might require a new understanding of tradition. Even so, the principle remains: regret that weighs down the spirit can hinder personal growth and social harmony. By addressing it openly, we can find a balance between respecting cultural values and preserving our mental well-being.

People who release regret often report a surge of gratitude for the present. Freed from obsessing over what could have been, they notice small joys again. They appreciate the people around them. They become aware that time is passing, and they do not wish to waste more of it in remorse. This grateful mindset can deepen connections. It can also inspire them to seize opportunities that arise now. They might start a new hobby or reconnect with old friends. They might volunteer, feeling that life is a gift to be shared. This shift from regret to gratitude can be one of the most profound outcomes of the healing process.

Yet, we must not rush the process. Telling someone to "just get over it" can do more harm. Regret often holds layers of emotion. We might need time to grieve the loss of a dream or to process shame. We might also need therapy if regret is tied to trauma. Each step demands patience. In some cases, journaling helps. Putting thoughts on paper can reveal patterns and triggers. It can also mark progress as we see how our mindset changes over weeks or months. Another method is seeking advice from those who have gone through similar regrets and emerged stronger. Their stories can offer guidance. They show that healing is possible, even if the path is not simple.

Regret sometimes flares up unexpectedly. We think we have let something go, and then a memory resurfaces. This can happen on an anniversary or when we hear a certain song. Such moments do not mean we have failed to release regret. They might just be reminders that healing is not a straight line. Each time, we can practice the same steps of acknowledgment and self-compassion. Over time, these flare-ups become less intense. We might even use them as prompts to reflect on how far we have come. We see that the pain is not as sharp, or that we recover faster. That recognition brings confidence.

On a larger scale, societies that encourage open dialogue about regret might see less stigma around failure. People might speak honestly about missteps, sharing what they learned. Leaders could hold public discussions on national or historical regrets, leading to more transparency and growth. This approach counters the tendency to hide failures out of shame. It can also encourage creative solutions to ongoing problems. When mistakes are not seen as final condemning marks, communities can try new ideas without crippling fear. That culture shift can make it easier for everyone to release personal regret since they know they are part of a broader environment that values learning.

Releasing regret can also tie to the concept of humility. When we let go of regret, we admit we are not perfect. We see we have made misjudgments, but that does not define us. This humility can make us kinder to others who err. We do not rush to judge them, because we recall our regrets. This fosters a more supportive atmosphere. It can also deepen friendships. When two people share their regrets openly and support each other, they forge strong bonds. They stand as reminders that no one is alone in feeling remorse. That sense of community can be a powerful antidote to isolation or despair.

The very act of releasing regret can spark a renewed sense of purpose. We might realize that the time spent lamenting the past can now be used to contribute positively. We could volunteer, mentor youth, or start a small initiative in our neighborhood. Feeling free from regret's chains can encourage us to help others break theirs. We see how big a difference it makes to face regrets head-on, and we want to share that discovery. Such endeavors can also bring more meaning to our lives, refilling the emotional gaps regret once occupied. Over time, we gain new memories that overshadow the old disappointments.

In the end, releasing regret does not erase what happened. It does not rewrite history or promise a perfect future. It does, however, change our relationship to the past. It shifts our perspective from helpless shame to active growth. It turns a heavy weight into a stepping stone. That is the core of its importance. Without letting go, we remain bound to old stories, reliving them over and over. With the release, we step into new possibilities. We might still feel a trace of sadness at times, but it no longer crushes us. We carry the lessons and move forward. As this journey continues, we might find that regret transforms into compassion for ourselves and others. In that compassion, we discover a well of peace that regret once hid from view. That peace, in turn, enriches all that we do. And this is why releasing regret stands as a vital step on the path to inner peace.

14. Harmony Within

Harmony within can feel like a gentle breeze that calms the storm in your mind. It does not mean you never get upset. It does not mean you float through life with no challenges. Instead, it means you carry a sense of balance inside you. You can face daily problems without being pulled apart by them. You can find peace even when events do not go your way. This quality comes from cultivating a steady core. It grows when you respect your feelings and remain open to others. At times, it feels like a soft glow in the heart, guiding you toward kinder words and calmer actions. It helps you step back when arguments flare. It reminds you to breathe and seek common ground. In this sense, harmony within is not just a private matter. It shapes your relationships and your choices. You become less likely to snap at someone or hold onto grudges. You see each moment as a chance to bring clarity instead of confusion. Over time, this practice can change how you see yourself and the world. You begin to trust that, beneath all the noise, a quiet center remains. You learn that you can return to it again and again, no matter what is happening. This trust forms the basis of inner harmony. It is not flashy or dramatic. It is subtle, yet powerful. It allows you to be present for life's ups and downs without losing yourself. That presence can lift your mood, improve your health, and enhance your connections. It can also influence how you respond to conflict in your community or workplace. It might even spark a sense of purpose, as you realize how your calm approach can benefit others. It becomes clear that harmony within is not a selfish goal. It is a foundation that lets you serve the greater good in a more balanced way.

The social impact of inner harmony can be surprising. People who have found some balance often spread that peace to those around them. Their friends might notice they do not escalate arguments. They do not jump to blame or shame. Instead, they listen with patience. This listening can defuse tension. When a tense situation arises, a harmonious person steps in calmly. They do not deny the problem. They just do not add fuel to it. Neighbors might see this calm approach and adopt it themselves. Over time, small pockets of harmony can develop in a community. Conflicts might not disappear, but they are handled with greater respect. People are less reactive. They are less consumed by grudges. They focus on solutions rather than scoring points. This shift can affect entire neighborhoods or even larger groups. It might lead to more effective discussions on local issues. It might encourage volunteer projects that bridge divides. On a family level, harmony within one member can change the household tone. Children learn that emotions can be managed without yelling or slamming doors. They see an example of balanced responses. As they grow, they carry these habits into their friendships. They become less likely to bully or mock others. They learn that empathy is possible even when people disagree. All of this begins with one person choosing to nurture inner harmony. Of course, that choice is not always easy. Stress can tempt anyone to lash out or withdraw. But if we return to that quiet center, we remember that calm is within reach. This knowledge helps us keep trying. It reminds us that small acts of kindness, gentleness, or patience ripple outward in ways we might never fully see.

The importance of harmony within becomes clear when we look at our mental and physical health. Constant stress takes a toll on the body. It can raise blood pressure, strain the heart, and weaken the immune system. It can also cloud the mind with worry or agitation. When we work toward inner harmony, we counter some of these effects. We give the body a chance to relax and recover. That does not mean we avoid all stress. Life is full of demands. But we learn to return to a calm baseline more quickly. We avoid carrying tension in our muscles for hours or days. We practice releasing the mental clutter that keeps us awake at night. Over time, this can improve sleep, digestion, and overall well-being. Emotionally, inner harmony reduces the grip of panic or hopelessness. We see that circumstances will keep shifting, yet we have a stable core inside. This helps us handle surprises without collapsing. We become more resilient. We also become more available to others who need support. If we are consumed by turmoil, it is hard to give much attention to a friend in need. But if we have a level of calm, we can be present. This presence can be a great gift, both for ourselves and those we care about. Our capacity for compassion grows when we are not lost in our distress. This is another reason why harmony within matters so much. It is not about ignoring our difficulties. It is about meeting them with a steady heart.

Challenges arise when people try to find harmony within. Some worry it means becoming passive or indifferent. But true harmony does not involve ignoring problems. It involves seeing them clearly and responding from a place of balance. Another challenge is the fast pace of modern life. Many of us race from one task to another. We seldom pause. Our minds jump from phone notifications to social media feeds to deadlines. This environment makes it hard to cultivate calm. We might need to set boundaries, like turning off devices at certain times or scheduling quiet breaks. Another obstacle is the emotional baggage we carry from childhood. We might have learned patterns of stress or anger from family. Changing these deep-seated habits takes effort and patience. We might slip back into old reactions during tough moments. That can be discouraging. But progress often comes in small steps. Each time we catch ourselves and return to a calmer response, we strengthen the new habit. Over weeks or months, that habit becomes more natural. A further challenge is that some people fear to calm themselves. They find it uncomfortable because chaos feels familiar. Letting go of drama can leave them feeling empty. Learning to appreciate stillness can take time. We might start by noticing small joys in quiet moments. Over time, these joys become more appealing than the rush of conflict.

One lesser-known fact about harmony within is how it can boost creativity. When the mind is stormy with tension, it is harder to see fresh ideas. Stress narrows our vision, focusing on threats or tasks. But a calm mind can wander in healthy ways. It can form unexpected connections or dream up novel solutions. Many artists, writers, and scientists speak of their best insights arriving when they are relaxed. That does not mean they are lazy. It means their minds are free from constant worry. Inner harmony can create that mental openness. Another fascinating point is how harmony within can shape our decision-making. We are less likely to make impulsive choices when we feel balanced. We can weigh the pros and cons without being hijacked by fear or desire. This measured approach often leads to better outcomes. We might also become more ethical in our decisions, as we pause to consider the impact on others. Harmony fosters empathy and clarity, both of which guide thoughtful action. This can matter greatly in leadership roles. A leader who remains calm in crisis can keep a team steady. They avoid panic-based moves. They also encourage trust. People sense that the leader is grounded, not flailing. This dynamic can ripple throughout an organization, improving morale and cooperation.

Harmony within also has a spiritual dimension for many. Different cultures and faiths speak of an inner peace that aligns us with a larger reality. Some call it divine presence. Others describe it as cosmic unity or simply the depth of being. The words vary, yet the experience is similar. There is a sense of calm that embraces existence as it is. Anxiety about the future or guilt about the past fades. In such moments, we might feel connected to something vast yet comforting. Even those who are not religious can experience a profound awe or sense of unity. This can occur when walking in nature, gazing at the night sky, or simply sitting quietly. Cultivating harmony can increase these moments. We become more aware of life's wonders when we are not tangled in stress. This awareness can lead to gratitude. That gratitude, in turn, reinforces our calm. We see the gifts around us, even if life is not perfect.

Social media can either support or undermine harmony within. On one hand, it can connect us with mindfulness tips or like-minded communities. We can find guided meditations or encouraging posts. On the other hand, it can stir envy, outrage, or endless comparisons. We might need to set limits or choose our online content carefully. Another modern issue is the push toward constant productivity. Many workplaces reward those who never seem to rest. People brag about how busy they are. This culture can exhaust our nervous system. Seeking inner harmony might require reevaluating such norms. We might decide that downtime is essential, not a luxury. We might also advocate for healthier workplace policies. This shift can bring conflict if the environment values hustle above all. Yet, it can also plant seeds of change, as others realize the benefit of balance.

One might ask how to begin finding harmony within. A common approach is mindfulness. We pause during the day and notice our breath. We see if our body is tense. We scan for clenched jaws or hunched shoulders. We consciously relax them. We might also watch our thoughts without getting lost in them. This practice can be done in small moments, like waiting in line or sitting on the bus. Another approach is journaling. We can write about what upsets us and see patterns in our triggers. Over time, we learn to respond differently. Some people find nature walks calming. Others prefer yoga or martial arts that combine movement with focus. The key is to find a method that resonates and stick with it. No single path works for everyone. The consistent effort to return to calm can retrain the mind. The mind learns that there is a gentle place to rest, even amid busy days.

Laughter can also be a tool for harmony. When we laugh, tension breaks. We see the lighter side of a problem. We bond with others in shared amusement. This is not about mocking serious issues. It is about allowing humor to ease the heaviness. Similarly, acts of kindness can nurture inner peace. Helping someone can shift our focus from worry to compassion. That shift reduces self-centered rumination. We realize the world is bigger than our troubles. This perspective supports a balanced mind. Another helpful practice is gratitude. Listing a few things we are thankful for each day can reframe our mindset. It highlights abundance rather than lack. It does not solve every concern, but it brightens our outlook.

Harmony within also shows its worth during conflicts. We might disagree with someone about politics, religion, or personal matters. If we come from a place of inner calm, we can listen deeply. We can speak honestly without attacking. This reduces the chance of escalation. We might still fail to see eye to eye, but we preserve respect. Over time, such respectful communication can build bridges. It might lead to surprising agreements or compromises. Even when it does not, we walk away without hatred. That alone is a victory in a world filled with division. Harmony within helps us recognize that arguments do not have to be personal wars. They can be exchanges of views between equals, each with dignity. This approach can defuse tension in families, offices, and communities.

Another aspect of harmony within involves how we handle mistakes. We might slip and say something hurtful in a moment of anger. If we maintain some calm, we notice the error sooner. We can apologize sincerely and correct ourselves. We do not spiral into shame or denial. We do not lash out again in defense. Over time, this builds integrity. People see that we are willing to admit faults and grow. This can earn trust. It also prevents small errors from turning into bigger conflicts. Of course, it is not easy to stay calm when criticized. The ego wants to push back. But with practice, we get better at pausing and breathing before responding. That small pause can change everything. It allows the mind to catch up with the heart. We remember that harmony is possible if we choose it.

In personal relationships, harmony within can prevent codependency or constant drama. We do not rely on the other person to fix all our moods. We handle our stress through healthy means. We can still lean on loved ones for support. Yet, we remain aware that they are not responsible for our inner state. This fosters a healthier bond. It reduces fights about trivial things. We also become more empathetic listeners. We give our partners room to be themselves without drowning them in our emotional swings. This dynamic can strengthen the sense of closeness and respect. It can also help children who witness such interactions learn healthier emotional coping. They grow up seeing that calm conversation is normal, and that shouting is not the default.

There is a little-known link between harmony within and how we experience time. When anxious, we often feel rushed. Minutes slip away as we fret. But with inner calm, time seems to expand. We notice details, like the taste of food or the sound of birds. We become more fully alive at each moment. This can improve our memory since we are present for events. It can also sharpen our work performance. Instead of multitasking in a panic, we focus on one thing at a time. The quality of our output often rises. People sometimes discover that by slowing down internally, they get more done. They waste less energy on worry or mental clutter. This is not about laziness. It is about mindful action.

Cultivating harmony within also influences how we see ourselves. We might realize that we do not need to be perfect or extraordinary at all times. We learn to be kind to our flaws. We see them as part of being human, not as reasons for self-loathing. That kindness can reduce depression or self-criticism. In turn, it can encourage us to improve gently. We no longer push ourselves with harsh demands. Instead, we guide ourselves with compassion. We might still set goals or strive for growth, but we do so without tearing ourselves down. This approach can boost self-esteem in a steady, realistic manner.

Some might think harmony within means never feeling negative emotions. That is not accurate. Emotions come and go. Even the calmest person can feel sadness, anger, or fear. The difference is that they do not get swept away. They observe the emotion, accept it, and let it pass. They do not cling to it or blow it up. This skill can be learned. It helps us maintain balance even in emotional storms. We do not suppress what we feel, but we also do not let it control our every move. This approach can reduce impulsive actions we might later regret. It can also help us empathize with others who are in emotional turmoil. We see that their outburst might be a passing wave, not their true self.

In a broader sense, harmony within can become a guiding principle. We can ask ourselves, "Does this choice increase or decrease my sense of peace?" That question can steer us away from toxic relationships or environments. It can help us choose a job that aligns with our values rather than one that pays more but causes constant stress. It can guide us to healthier hobbies, meaningful friendships, and balanced schedules. Gradually, these choices shape a life that fosters inner calm. We might discover we do not need as much clutter or drama as we once believed. We might find simpler joys that bring genuine satisfaction. This transformation can even ripple into bigger life changes, like moving to a quieter place or shifting careers. As we grow more in tune with calm, we notice what disrupts it. We then seek ways to reduce those disruptions while respecting our responsibilities.

When people come together with a shared commitment to inner harmony, their collective energy shifts. Meetings might run more smoothly. School events might have less tension. Neighbors might band together for community projects without petty rivalries. This does not mean a conflict-free utopia, but it does mean challenges are addressed with cooler heads. People can compromise more willingly. They can accept differences while focusing on mutual goals. Over time, this can reduce violence or hostility. Even if conflicts arise, they are approached with a sense of shared respect. Each person tries to maintain their internal balance rather than letting anger take over. This cultural shift might seem small, but it has the power to reshape how groups function. It can build trust where suspicion used to reign.

Harmony within also helps us handle unexpected crises. Life can throw sudden losses, accidents, or global disasters at us. Those who have practiced calm are less likely to panic. They can keep their composure, assist others, and find solutions. This does not mean they do not feel fear or sadness. It means they do not drown in those feelings. They can keep their perspective and adapt. This resilience can save lives in emergencies. It can also help entire communities recover faster. People who remain centered can organize relief efforts, comfort those who are grieving, and keep morale up. They can also deal with the aftermath of trauma in healthier ways. They do not bury the pain, but they do not let it paralyze them either.

Ultimately, harmony within is about fostering a peaceful home inside oneself. It is not a final state we achieve once and for all. It is a living practice that we nurture daily. We may slip at times. We might have days or weeks where stress wins. But each time we notice, we can return to that soft center. We can remind ourselves that calm is a choice, not a luxury. In doing so, we fill our lives with gentler energy. This energy radiates through our words, actions, and even our silence. It benefits loved ones, strangers, and our health. It supports wise decision-making, open-minded dialogue, and heartfelt empathy. It can also deepen our sense of wonder at life itself. When the mind quiets, we become aware of details we used to overlook. We notice the subtle colors of a sunset or the kindness in a stranger's smile. Harmony within awakens us to the beauty around and within us.

In the end, harmony within is not about perfection. It is about sincerity in our efforts. It is about remembering that we hold a calm space inside, even when outer conditions swirl. We can learn to step into that space when needed. We can also carry its essence into our busy routines. We can let it inform how we speak to a coworker or how we handle a rude driver. Each time we act from that place, we strengthen it. We remind ourselves that peace can be active, not passive. It can be a stance of quiet strength rather than weakness. When enough people in a family, community, or even the world choose this path, a larger shift can happen. Disagreements might still arise, but they no longer escalate so easily. Fears might still visit us, but they do not lock us in panic. Mistakes might still occur, but they become lessons rather than permanent sources of shame. In short, harmony within can set a tone for how life unfolds. It can turn daily living into an ongoing practice of balance and kindness, both to ourselves and those we meet along the way. That gentle power can shape us, heal us, and remind us that inner peace is possible, even in a complex world.

A peaceful journey can mean different things to different people. For some, it is a trip through quiet forests or along calm rivers. For others, it is a state of mind that follows them wherever they go. But at its heart, a peaceful journey is an experience of moving through life with less conflict, less stress, and more awareness. It means choosing a path that does not rely on constant anxiety or aggression. It means finding ways to travel—both physically and emotionally—without bringing chaos into every moment. That choice is not always easy. It often involves careful thought about how we deal with challenges. It can also involve big or small changes in how we interact with others. Yet, the reward is a deeper sense of calm. It is a sense that, no matter the bumps in the road, we carry peace within us. That peace then shapes each step, each conversation, and each rest stop along the way.

A peaceful journey does not hide from real problems. It does not deny that difficulties exist. On the contrary, it encourages us to address them with a calm mind and a steady heart. It shows us that we do not need to run or panic when things go wrong. We can pause, breathe, and look for a balanced response. This does not guarantee we always succeed. But it shifts our default reaction. It allows us to engage with issues instead of being overwhelmed. Over time, this approach can reduce the stress that builds when we resist or avoid obstacles. The journey becomes less about always feeling perfect and more about consistently returning to a calmer perspective. By doing so, we discover that storms can pass. We do not have to cling to fear or anger. We can observe those emotions, learn from them, and then let them go. That process helps keep our inner compass directed toward peace, even in rough weather.

This idea of a peaceful journey holds a social impact. People who practice this way of moving through life often radiate calm to those around them. Their families might notice fewer arguments or less tension. Their workplaces might benefit from more thoughtful communication. Over time, such an attitude can spread through small acts. A single person who handles conflict with composure can influence a team. That team might start adopting calmer methods. This ripple effect can continue outward. Neighbors might see the difference and become inspired. Children who grow up around it might learn that shouting and blaming are not the only options. They might see that it is possible to solve problems through patient listening and cooperation. This can reduce aggression at school or in social settings. It can also encourage creative problem-solving. When fear and anger are not always at the forefront, new solutions have space to appear. That can improve many relationships, from close friendships to community links. A peaceful journey, in that sense, does not stay private. It finds ways to enrich the larger world.

The importance of choosing such a path becomes clearer when we look at the toll that conflict and stress can take. Many suffer from anxiety that drains their energy. They might carry a weight of constant worry, always expecting the worst. That mindset affects their health, their work, and their personal lives. By setting the intention to walk more calmly, people can guard their mental and physical well-being. The body reacts to stress with tense muscles, high blood pressure, and a flood of stress hormones. Over long periods, this can lead to chronic conditions. A peaceful journey helps counteract that harmful cycle. It does not eliminate every stressful event, but it teaches a healthier response. Instead of letting stress accumulate, we learn to acknowledge it and then release it. This can promote better sleep, improved immune function, and a more stable mood. It can also boost concentration since a calmer mind wastes less time on frantic thoughts.

A peaceful journey also shapes how we manage challenges. We still experience tough choices, setbacks, or sudden changes. But we approach them with less panic and more problem-solving. We do not ignore strong emotions. We simply do not let them hijack our entire process. This steadiness can be particularly valuable in group settings. When multiple people are upset, a calm presence can anchor the discussion. It can remind everyone that clarity is possible. Over time, this approach builds trust. People see that we do not react wildly or lash out when under pressure. That trust can lead to more cooperation. It can also pave the way for deeper bonds. And from those bonds, new forms of support might arise. Perhaps coworkers become more willing to help each other. Perhaps neighbors start sharing resources. Each small shift can contribute to a broader sense of peace.

Of course, this journey does not come without challenges. Some might think a peaceful journey is naive. They assume that life requires constant struggle or fierce competition. They might see calmness as a weakness. Overcoming that assumption can be hard. We might face criticism from those who prefer harsher tactics. We might also battle our doubts because part of us might believe that aggression is the only way to get results. Another challenge is that old habits die hard. If we have spent years reacting with anger or fear, changing that pattern takes conscious effort. We might slip back into shouting or sulking when triggered. That does not mean we have failed. It means we are human. The peaceful journey is about ongoing practice, not sudden perfection. Each slip can teach us more about our triggers and how to handle them next time.

Another challenge is external pressure from fast-paced environments. We live in a culture that values instant gratification. Many expect quick answers or immediate compliance. In that rush, calm can feel like a luxury. We might get swept along by deadlines or social media feeds. We might believe we have no time to pause and breathe. Yet, ironically, a brief pause often improves productivity. A moment of reflection can clarify our goals and refine our actions. This means that continuing a peaceful journey in a high-speed world can demand mindful scheduling. We might need to schedule breaks or set limits on screen time. We might also need to practice saying no to commitments that overload us. This can be tough if we feel pressured to always say yes. But part of the journey is learning that boundaries preserve our well-being. Without them, stress will build up until it overwhelms us.

Some lesser-known facts about a peaceful journey can inspire us to stay on this path. Research shows that people who maintain calm under stress often perform better on cognitive tasks. Their decision-making is more accurate and less influenced by fleeting emotions. Another interesting point is that peace can be contagious. When one person remains composed in a heated debate, others sometimes start mirroring that calm. They lower their voices. They consider fresh viewpoints. This shift might not always be immediate, but it happens enough to be noticeable. Additionally, certain cultures have long traditions of peaceful journeys. For instance, some indigenous communities teach that the land and the people are interconnected. They see that harming one part harms the whole. This idea extends beyond environmental concerns. It suggests that aggression and conflict also damage the larger web of life. Those teachings can remind us that a peaceful path benefits everyone, not just the individual.

The social benefits of a peaceful journey can take many forms. One form is conflict resolution without violence. People who value calm might step in to mediate between feuding neighbors or feuding political groups. They listen to both sides, ensuring each party feels heard. This can reduce tension before it escalates. Another form is community projects that focus on shared well-being. When a group commits to problem-solving with respect, they find common ground more easily. They might decide to build a community garden or start a local tutoring program. These efforts can strengthen bonds. They also shift the focus from personal feuds to constructive goals. Over time, such activities can transform the local atmosphere. They show that peace is not about ignoring problems. It is about facing them with thoughtful cooperation.

On a personal level, a peaceful journey can enhance relationships. Friends might enjoy our company more if we are not constantly upset. We might have fewer arguments with our partners or relatives. In times of disagreement, we handle it with curiosity rather than hostility. That does not mean we never get irritated. We still have preferences, and we still argue. But we learn to argue without tearing each other down. That skill alone can save countless hours of emotional drama. It can also make love stronger, as each person feels safer to express themselves without fear of a harsh attack. In workplaces, the peaceful approach can lower stress for everyone. Meetings can be more productive when calm voices prevail. Colleagues might share ideas more openly if they sense no one will mock them. This can boost innovation and morale. Managers who practice calm leadership can inspire loyalty. Their team sees they do not panic in crises. That confidence can spread, giving the entire organization a more stable foundation.

The value of a peaceful journey extends to the global scale. Many conflicts in the world persist because people fuel them with anger, fear, or revenge. If more individuals approached differences with calm readiness to listen, large-scale tensions might ease. This is not a quick fix for all problems. But it sets a tone that encourages diplomacy and dialogue. Leaders who keep their composure can guide nations through disputes without resorting to violence. Citizens who support peaceful policies can demand that their representatives find humane solutions. This does not mean being naive about threats or injustice. It means addressing them in ways that seek reconciliation, not endless retaliation. Over time, this can help regions move from conflict to gradual peace.

At the same time, a peaceful journey does not ignore the need for firm boundaries. There are moments when we must protect ourselves or others from harm. The difference is that we can do so without hate in our hearts. We can set a boundary calmly, stating that certain behavior is not acceptable. We do not need to respond with cruelty or fury.

This approach can be seen in some nonviolent movements throughout history. People stood against oppression firmly but did not let hatred consume them. That stance can shift social structures while preserving dignity. It might not always succeed instantly. But it offers a path that aligns with the values of respect and empathy.

The personal challenges on this path can still be intense. Old habits of reacting with anger or worry can be stubborn. We might also find certain triggers that set us off, such as a rude driver or a disappointing work evaluation. In those moments, the peaceful journey calls for self-awareness. We notice the rush of adrenaline or the tightening in our chest. We pause, if only for a second, to breathe. We remember our intention to choose calm. Then we decide how to respond. Maybe we speak up firmly but not cruelly. Maybe we let a small annoyance go, knowing it is not worth the stress. Over time, these small decisions add up. They form a new pattern in the mind and body. They show us that we are capable of traveling through life with more grace.

Some might believe that a peaceful journey is dull or lacks excitement. They might think drama is what makes life interesting. But peace does not mean boredom. It means freedom from unnecessary turmoil. It means we can still experience excitement, adventure, and even passionate debates, yet we handle them from a centered place. We can still climb mountains, start businesses, or pursue artistic dreams with great energy. The difference is that we do not cling to stress as our default. We can handle intense situations while staying present, not letting our minds spiral. This presence can heighten our enjoyment. We become more aware of details, more attuned to beauty, more connected to others. That can feel richer than constant drama ever could.

The peaceful journey also influences how we treat ourselves. We might become kinder to our bodies, eating more mindfully rather than stress-eating junk food. We might exercise without punishing ourselves. We might sleep better, knowing we have done our best for the day. We also become kinder to our minds. We notice self-criticism and replace it with understanding. We see that harsh inner talk only creates more inner conflict. Instead, we encourage ourselves gently, the way we would support a friend. That self-kindness builds resilience. When we do face failure or rejection, we can recover faster. We do not wallow in shame as long. We pick ourselves up and continue, still guided by calm.

A peaceful journey can also unlock creativity. By reducing mental static, we open space for ideas to flow. We might write, paint, or solve problems in new ways. We might find that calm fosters insight. It does not mean we never struggle with creative blocks. But we might handle them with patience. We do not panic when inspiration stalls. We wait, experiment, or switch tasks, trusting that a fresh idea will emerge. This sense of trust grows from inner calm. It says that we do not have to force everything. Sometimes, letting the mind rest invites clarity. The same principle can apply to any field, from science to business. A calmer approach can lead to breakthrough solutions that frantic efforts might miss.

We can start this journey at any time. Perhaps we read an article about mindfulness or we recall a friend who seemed genuinely peaceful. We feel inspired. Our next step could be to try a simple breathing exercise each morning. Or we might decide to apologize to someone we fought with, aiming to clear the air. We might read a book on stress management, or we might seek therapy to address deeper anxiety. Each person's path will differ. The key is consistent effort. A single day of calm does not fix everything. But day by day, our mindset changes. We find we have more control over our reactions. We also begin to see that we are not alone. Others around us might also be seeking a gentler existence. We can encourage one another, share tips, or form small communities focused on mental well-being. Even in modern life, where distractions abound, such circles can thrive.

Sometimes, the journey calls us to reflect on what truly matters. We realize that chasing every external validation or every shiny gadget does not bring lasting contentment. We might choose to simplify or declutter our lives. We might opt for meaningful connections over superficial ones. This does not require extreme measures. It can be as basic as spending more time with loved ones instead of scrolling aimlessly online. It can involve giving back to the community. It can also spark gratitude for small blessings, like a sunny day or a warm meal. That gratitude feeds the sense of peace within. It reminds us that life holds beauty, even in difficult times.

Of course, adversity will come. We might lose a job, or a friendship might end. We might face illness or financial setbacks. A peaceful journey does not shield us from all pain. But it can offer a framework for moving through sorrow or fear with a measure of calm. We do not deny the hurt. We allow ourselves to feel it. Yet, we also trust that we can cope. We do not collapse into despair, nor do we pretend all is fine. We hold the truth of the pain and the truth of our inner strength at the same time. That balance can guide us to seek help if needed. It can also keep us from harming ourselves or others out of desperation. Over time, we heal more stably. We rejoin life's flow without being consumed by bitterness.

A peaceful journey also reveals that we can act without aggression. Some assume that to fight injustice, we must use anger or violence. But many examples in history show that calm determination can achieve great change. Nonviolent movements have toppled oppressive systems. Patient dialogue has ended wars. Compassionate negotiation has resolved longstanding feuds. These successes required courage and resilience, but not brutality. They show that harmony and firmness can coexist. We can stand up for what is right while still maintaining respect for opponents. This is not always simple. Yet, it offers a path that avoids the endless cycle of revenge. It aligns with the values of empathy and dignity. By following such examples, our peaceful journey might inspire bigger shifts in how we engage with society's problems.

In conclusion, a peaceful journey is more than just an abstract idea. It is a daily practice of choosing calm, respect, and understanding whenever possible. It influences our well-being, our friendships, our families, and even our broader communities. It can lead to improved health, reduced conflict, and deeper connections. It teaches us to navigate life's storms without sinking into panic or resentment. It shows that we can pursue our goals, stand up for our beliefs, and remain grounded. Though challenges will arise, each step on this path strengthens our ability to respond with clarity. Over time, it becomes second nature to approach difficulties from a place of balance. This journey may stretch throughout our entire lifetime. But each phase brings new insights and fresh reasons to continue. We see that peace is not the absence of all problems. It is the presence of a calm heart ready to face them. And that calm heart, nurtured by daily choices and mindful actions, is the cornerstone of a truly peaceful journey.

• • • •

• • • •

www.ingramcontent.com/pod-product-compliance
Ingram Content Group UK Ltd.
Pitfield, Milton Keynes, MK11 3LW, UK
UKHW040957030225
454602UK00001B/84

9 798230 613374